Accidental Friends

Chapter 1
Two Dumps and a Rorschach

I was not under arrest and yet the interrogator would hold up an 11 X 14 inch card and ask me what I saw. The cards had ink spilled or splashed onto them. Some of the blots formed symmetrical images, some asymmetrical. I was instructed to report my initial impressions. If nothing came to mind I was instructed to fabricate a story. The stories didn't have to make sense. They didn't have to have a beginning, an end, or even a plot. The impressions and stories were for the interrogator to interpret. It was the Rorschach Ink Blot Test. The stories and impressions unconsciously revealed personality traits, desires and concerns. I likened the test to dream interpretation except that I was awake and (un)consciously fabricating the stories.

I can't remember a single story for cards one through fifteen, but I have never forgotten the projection for card 16. Unlike the previous 15 cards, card 16 was blank (completely white). The story was of a skier in a snow storm. The visibility was poor but the skier was racing down a double black diamond run full of moguls. Along with the colorful description of the skier's clothing the skier was in complete control on the run, hands in front, well balanced, knees bent to absorb shock and feet four to six inches apart. The feelings attached to the skier were of someone working hard to accomplish something difficult rather than those attached to an expert skier happily cruising down a tough run to impress the ski bunnies.

The interrogator, one of my favorite college professors, identified change and ambition as the recurring themes elicited during the Rorschach. I definitely had ambition and the changes that accompany graduating college were rapidly approaching. She and my other favorite Psychology professor agreed to write letters of recommendation for graduate school psychology programs. But, both professors recommended that I go to Medical School or do research instead of clinical psychology (counselling). They commented how much I would hate clinical psychology: "You'll sit in your office all day listening to people complain about problems that are easily solved. Most people who seek counseling don't want their problems solved, they only want someone to listen and sympathize." Sympathy and compassion? My wife still calls me "Mr. Compassionate".

When I did not receive admission to a Doctoral program in Psychology I had to make some big decisions. As I was evaluating a different professional direction, my personal direction also needed re-evaluation. I was two years into dating a sweet bubbly young woman who was going to be a grade school teacher. She graduated the year before and took a job teaching English to six year-olds in a developing country. She was not sure where her life was going but after nine months of "radio" silence (no phone calls or letters) I was sure that it was not with me. This was the no closure dump of disgrace: no discussion, no apology, and no explanation.

Turbo, one of my college roommates and best friends, recommended that I work for a year to gain some financial stability. Turbo's grandmother was the President of a regional jewelry firm with 12 stores. The first Holiday season he was in college he asked if I needed to earn some extra cash driving the delivery truck from the home office to a few of the stores. One year later I was selling diamonds and gold on the sales floor. I was no longer a calculus tutor making $3.15 per hour but a salesman making $9.00 an hour plus commission. Thanks to Turbo I moved from just below the poverty line to just above it.

In addition to the employment assistance, Turbo introduced me to one of his classmates. Madison was hormonally unbalanced, yet very pleasing to the eyeballs. We had a great first year together. When the fever hit, the emotions went non-linear. The rollercoaster ride of emotional volatility, known as Engagement Fever, started shortly after one of her roommates got engaged. They scoured bridal magazines looking at wedding dresses. Travel magazines were used to identify potential honeymoon destinations. She was obsessed with wedding day planning, and not just for her roommate. One day, out of nowhere, she decided that we should elope. We had been water skiing with friends at the lake. The day was over, the car was packed, and we were heading back to school when the fever hit. She decided that we should just drive to

Las Vegas and get married. Not that school or work
the next day mattered, it had to happen that night.
Fortunately, she had left her purse with photo ID in
the dorms and you can't get married without an ID or
a birth certificate. By the time we got home the fever
broke and the elopement was postponed. As part of
the appeasement package she agreed to let me buy
her an engagement ring. After all, I was managing a
jewelry store at the time. How ironic would it have
been if we got married or engaged without a ring? I
also mentioned that we might want to consider
asking for her father's permission to marry in case she
should change her mind about the elopement. She
was socially competitive so an extravagant ceremony
to impress her girlfriends was expected. I could
afford an elopement, maybe even a Honeymoon in
Vegas, but a big wedding and an international
vacation would mean significant financial and
emotional stress. Either that or acquiesce under her
father's financial thumb.

The following week she came by the store for lunch
and the ring selection ceremony. She walked in from
the parking lot and waited outside. We went to lunch
at the restaurant next door. She was quiet, almost
distracted. She barely touched her food. Eye contact
was at a minimum. She had every right to be
nervous. Getting married was something she
dreamed about since being a little girl. In a few
minutes the probability of realizing that dream would
be astronomically higher. My proposal was for her to
pick out three acceptable designs. I would then

secretly choose the one I liked the most, enlarge the size of the center stone, send off for the employee price and surprise her with the new and improved version. As she had been looking at rings for months I wasn't surprised when it only took five minutes for her to identify a top three. I was a bit surprised at her facial expressions while trying them on. Unconsciously I wondered if she didn't like how the rings looked on her finger or was it that she didn't like the implication of a ring, my ring, being on her finger? As she departed, I knew that something was terribly wrong. I didn't even bother sending in the request for the employee discount. She ended the relationship that very night. At least I got an explanation for this dump.

Turns out that she and another Communications major had been working together on a class project. The late nights together for the previous 3-4 weeks provided them a very intimate environment. Unbeknownst to me, Prince Charming had ignited the emotional rollercoaster ride making his move the week before the elopement demand. Her roommates had been encouraging the hook-up and his follow-up proposition came the night before the ring ceremony. I knew that something was wrong but attributed the emotional volatility to school work and engagement fever. Madison didn't really want to dump me as much as she wanted the equivalent of a 1031 Real Estate transaction. She wanted all her capital gains from our relationship to be transferred to a richer institution located in a better neighborhood. She

wanted a social class trade up with no tax (or
emotional) consequences. Culturally and socially
they had a lot more in common than we did. She and
the Prince were from families two or three
socioeconomic classes above mine. I'm sure that the
excitement of a new relationship with a rich kid
seemed like a safe gamble at the time. She and Prince
Charming were planning careers in the glamorous
film industry. I was in retail. I had shallow pockets,
his were deep. He had a safety net that could have
saved the Titanic, I was constantly tightrope walking
on a thread of Nylon. She felt entitled to a certain
quality of life as her tax free monthly allowance in
college was over half my fulltime managerial wages.
Prince Charming was also on a lucrative family
payroll. When the stench of this dump evaporated, I
seized the opportunity to re-embrace poverty and go
back to school.

**The moral of the stories: dumps always
create the best flowers and opportunities, all
you have to do is garden well.**

Chapter 2
Fahrvergnugen and Foundations

Immediately after the Prince Charming Filmmaker dump I resigned from management, reapplied to Master's Programs in Psychology and returned to the sales floor. As advised, I changed from Clinical to Research Psychology. I took the required pre-med undergraduate classes in the morning, worked afternoons at the jewelry store and took graduate level psychology classes at night. It was in Biology 101 that I met Katrina Sanders and Joshua Marks. Katrina was a dangerously attractive member of the opposite sex: five foot six, thick golden brown hair, slender long legs and no trouble filling out a bikini. Her laugh brightened any room on any day. Katrina was an Art History major who, during the summers, traveled extensively in Europe to see famous paintings. The travel also allowed her to learn Spanish and French. The Art History major, extensive travel and language fluencies differentiated her from the other 90% of Biology and Chemistry undergraduates applying to Medical School. When we met she was in a long-term relationship with Tyson. Tyson was a divorced Gynecologist who also loved to travel. Tyson's bad habit of bringing his work home with him led to his divorce. He literally got caught with his finger in a pie on several occasions.

Katrina and I ate lunch together three days a week. One slice of cheese pizza and one scoop of vanilla ice cream. We'd park ourselves outside on sunny days.

On cold or rainy days we ate in the Student Union. One day she complained that her haircuts costed $40. I jokingly said that I could do a better job at half the price. After all, I was going to be a surgeon. Even though I cut her hair for free the next three years I still think I got the better end of the deal. I was in love with her and enjoyed her company. Besides, cutting hair was like ironing shirts and mowing the lawn. They all require energy to make something beautiful from something messy or chaotic. Accomplishing those tasks always elicited emotions similar to those attributed to the skier on Rorschach card 16. I have been forever grateful for Katrina's friendship and the trust she gave to me from day one. I guess that's what accidental friends do: they love you from day one and invest in your long term success as a person.

I was taking a Graduate statistics class in Psychology when I met Samantha. My mother worked for a ticket agency at the time and frequently received complementary tickets to Broadway musicals and rock concerts. When she scored a pair of Bruce Springsteen tickets I asked Samantha if she'd like to go to the concert. We had heard about "The Boss" but together probably couldn't name more than one or two of his songs. I picked her up in my Volkswagen Rabbit GTI and we headed off to the concert. Volkswagen had a marketing campaign at the time extolling Fahrvergnugen or "driving enjoyment". I always thought that Fahrvergnugen meant "Free Radio" as three of mine would eventually be stolen.

Samantha and I made small talk on the way to the concert. We had to park in an auxiliary lot across the highway as the concert sold all of their allotted 80,000 tickets. As we were walking towards the stadium someone offered us $500 for the tickets. I politely declined as our plan was to go to the concert and dinner afterwards. After the concert we got back to the car and the passenger side fly window was broken. The radio had been stolen. Like I said, "Fahrvergnugen". I shook my head in disgust, wiped the broken glass off her seat and took her out for dinner. She said that both events (not selling the tickets for much needed cash and not going ballistic over the vandalized car) gave her a sense of maturity that her previous boyfriend never exhibited. Having property stolen, like bicycles, radios and motorcycles, was commonplace in the Hood.

I would eventually find out that Samantha's previous boyfriend had a bad temper. After dating for two years in High School and three years in college she outgrew him. But he couldn't let go. His last words to her were: "Screw you", except he used the F-word. A few months after their break-up he was riding his bicycle down a steep hill when a car pulled out in front of him. He was pronounced dead before she would even find out what happened. She felt responsible and whenever she felt guilty, she would think of him. We had a great relationship until, unbeknownst to me, she read my journal. She became quiet and withdrawn, and I was very confused. I originally thought she was having another bout of depression. She then confessed to reading the journal.

Occasionally, writing in a journal helped solve a relationship problem. Some journal entries were very useful for decision making. One could rationally look at options, weigh consequences, and formulate a plan. Unfortunately, many entries were totally irrational, wild distortions of the truth. Many entries were irrational impressions like those generated by Rorschach images. That's why they are very entertaining to reread years later. I can't tell you how many millions of times I attributed one of my bad faults onto the woman I was dating. Freud identified that ego defense mechanism as projection. In journal writing, projection, displacement, and venting are often intertwined. It was easy to complain, criticize and blame others for my own perceived bad circumstances, especially when the probability of retaliation or a negative consequence was believed to be zero. Her first reading of the journal left her confused. How did I treat her so well yet write such bad things about her? As I continued to treat her well her cognitive dissonance dissipated. She agreed not to read the journal again and I agreed to hide it instead of having it on my desk. Curiosity got the best of her and three years later she read it again. Now I was the one confused and distrustful. After a third reading, the relationship was over. This was very disappointing as we were very compatible.

Joshua, like Katrina, had a boyfriend physician. Joshua had already finished a Master's Degree in

Clinical Psychology and was repeating the required courses for Medical School Admissions. His undergraduate grade point average (GPA) suffered while he enjoyed too many mind altering distractions. He claimed that coffee and nicotine were his only residual bad habits. Joshua and I were paired as Physics 101 lab partners as we were the two oldest students in the class. Right from the start we clicked. We talked at length about psychoanalysis and religions of the Far East. We both initially wanted to go to medical school to become Psychiatrists but knew we were going to be surgeons. We both had an abundance of confidence and ambition. Over the next three years we too became great friends.

Katrina was the one who informed me that Joshua also had a boyfriend doctor. She confessed that at one time she considered leaving Tyson so that we could date, but she thought that I was gay. Bewildered, I asked her what would have given her the impression that I was gay? She assumed that I was gay because I hung out with Joshua and that he was gay. "Joshua's not gay" I protested. "Oh yes he is" she exclaimed. Then one night Joshua brings his boyfriend to a party. I'll be damned, he was gay. After the party we were all pretty hungry so we went to The Jester a 24 hour hamburger joint. I only knew of the place because I used to go there with my dad. He would sometimes go in the middle of the night. Amazingly, we walked in right as he was ordering. Now Katrina and Joshua had never met my dad. He was 100% Hispanic and I only 50% with much lighter skin color. He had obviously been working late and was dressed homeless casual. Katrina and Joshua were horrified when I sat across from him and started speaking to him in Spanish. Thinking that I had either totally lost my mind or drank too much at the party they asked what I was doing. I invited them over, "Katrina, Joshua, I'd like you to meet my Dad, Pancho Sr.". Neither one believed it as I was known for playing practical jokes. We played the yes he is — no he's not game for 5 minutes. His food arrived and I whispered in Katrina's ear, "He's going to put ketchup and mustard on his fries." Sure enough, ketchup and mustard on the fries. Still no believers so I said, "OK, then how would I know that his social security number is: 502-44-2427?" He then pulled out his military ID to verify the name and numbers. I had to have it memorized to use on the military bases when we were growing up.

Having served in the Vietnam War my dad had also been to the Far East and Europe. He had been to many of the same places that Katrina and Joshua had visited. Joshua spoke of one trip he and his Sugar Daddy took to a small uncivilized village in Cambodia. They had their first and last experience of knowingly eating pork (which their religion frowned upon). The village elders decided to sacrifice a pig for their honored guests. After seeing the animal washed and "cleaned" with muddy river water he had to close his eyes and pinch his nose while eating his portion. Retelling the story made him cringe with disgust. We laughed so hard our stomachs hurt.

These crazy travel experiences distinguished Joshua from the traditional biology and chemistry majors applying for medical school. His Medical School applications spoke about integrating Buddhist philosophy with his traditional Jewish upbringing. It contrasted civilized with uncivilized life, complex modern living with the simplicity of tribal life. It was off the charts intriguing.

Katrina, Joshua and I all did well on the Medical College Aptitude Test (MCAT). Katrina was accepted to the Royale College of Physicians and Surgeons. I received acceptances from Royale and Evergreen Medical College. Joshua received acceptance letters from Cobalt School of Medicine and Evergreen. My application uniqueness was an extensive work history achieving management positions with several companies, an advanced degree in Psychology and a "disadvantaged" ethnicity. I declined the full scholarship offer from Royale to attend Evergreen. Evergreen had the better reputation for training Academic leaders.

Joshua's decision algorithm was much more complex. Joshua and his Sugar Daddy were both born right coasters. They had moved to the left coast to embrace a more socially progressive lifestyle. Their parents were traditional upper class East Coast conservatives. Joshua's father had graduated from Cobalt and was considered an expert in his field. He disapproved of Joshua's lifestyle, especially his use of recreational pharmaceuticals. By the time Joshua applied to Medical School he and Dr. Sugar Daddy had been a couple for 10 years. Many of their left coast friends had died from a new, then untreatable disease called Acute Immune Deficiency Syndrome (AIDS). So when the Sugar Daddy was offered an academic position at Cobalt, they said goodbye to their west coast ghosts and headed home.

Moral of the stories: learning from other people's experiences, rather than their journal entries, always broadens your perspective.

Chapter 3
Bucket Lists & Three Nippled Mexicans

Evergreen and Cobalt had different philosophies for training academic leaders. Cobalt mandated that all students take a required curriculum. Class attendance was required and weekly exams were standard. The pre-clinical curriculum had to be completed in two years or you were out. Evergreen's only requirements were that students pass the Board Exams when their pre-clinical coursework was finished and when their clinical rotations were done. Evergreen encouraged students to take fewer medical school courses per semester and complete their preclinical work at their own pace. The extra time could be used to take classes in other Graduate Schools, learn another language, start a business, work in a lab and/or facilitate an excellent quality of life.

I used the extra time to work in an orthopedic research laboratory and as a Graduate Resident Assistant (GRA). One beautiful spring day I was having lunch with Aimi, accidental friend number six, when an unexpected knock at the door occurred. Many of us hosted medical school interviewees during their campus visits. I was not scheduled to host anyone. Maximillian was originally scheduled to stay with another student but mistakenly showed up at my door. Aimi, suggested that he just stay with me. Welcome, accidental friend number 007. He realized he was at the wrong place but decided that the housing error could wait until after a game or two of hoops. I'd like to think that he chose Evergreen because of his stay with me but it was probably the great weather. You can't play basketball outside in January on the East coast or in the Mid-West. Every day after class we ran, biked, lifted weights, played basketball or racquetball.

Evergreen's roommate policy encouraged cross pollination of Graduate Students. All roommates were randomly assigned into Graduate housing. My roommate, Antonio, was an exchange student from Italy. He was the recipient of an Italian government scholarship to attend Evergreen for a one year Master's program. If he did not get accepted into the Physics PhD program on scholarship he would have to return to Italy. Although he was from Rome we told everyone that he was from Bologna so we could call him Tony Baloney. His first nine months at Evergreen consisted of eating, going to class, working in a lab, studying and sleeping. He was Tony no fun Baloney. A magical transformation occurred the day he was accepted into the PhD program. He went parasailing with his friends in the lab. He then started joining us on runs and bike rides.

During the summer between my first and second years I went to visit Maximillian in New York. One day we went downtown to meet one of his best friends and one of Aimi's college friends. We took the train in all agreeing to meet at Park and Fifth Avenues at 10 AM. We got off the train and navigated through thousands of busy important New Yorkers all in a rush to get some place else.

Maximillian could easily identify Cool Breeze but I had never met Huelo (pronounced You-low), all I had was Aimi's description: "A beautiful Polynesian babe." By the time we got to the meeting place Cool Breeze was leaning up against the street post putting the moves on Huelo. Maximillian had forwarded her description to him and he made sure he was going to get first chance to make an impression. She was wearing grey slacks, black boots, a black Tang suit with golden knot buttons and a Mandarin collar. Her hair was in a large braid and she had on reflective aviator sunglasses. She later told me that the Cool Breeze tried every cheesy pick up line on her he could think of.

The four of us went to the Museum of Modern Art then stopped for dinner near Wall Street. I asked Huelo if she was going to the Film Festival in Connecticut the next day as Aimi had a small short debuting. She said that she was between acting jobs and didn't want to spend the money. What little money she did have she planned to use for transportation to and from auditions. She was proud of the fact that she had never bused tables in New York. Her skills as an actress were paying the rent and putting food on the table. I offered to pay for her transportation and meals. With a little encouragement from Maximillian and the Cool Breeze, she agreed.

The next morning I arrived with luggage in tote and headed towards the ticket counter at Grand Central Station. It was like a scene from the movie:

The Fisher King. In the movie Robin Williams played Parry, a schizophrenic homeless man who secretly followed a woman to and from work. As Lydia walked across the Grand Central Station foyer beams of sunlight filtered through the roof, classical music played inside Parry's head and he imagined people waltzing through the terminal. The music and waltzing stopped when she exited the building. That morning, Huelo happened to be standing in the terminal center with a single beam of sunshine focused on her. She was wearing a bonnet with a lavender ribbon circling the hat and draping down 20 additional inches. Her long black hair was not braided like the day before but flowing gently in the breeze. No aviator sunglasses, her shirt was violet, shorts light blue, matching lavender socks and white tennis shoes. This experience was either heir Cupid striking me with a thunderbolt of love or my first schizophrenic delusion. After saying hello she said she'd like to buy a magazine for the train ride to Connecticut. She often used current events when auditioning for theatre roles. I had an eight pound biochemistry textbook for light reading but we ended up talking the entire trip. She later confessed that she wanted the magazine in case I was a dork and she no longer wanted to talk.

We had a great time and I headed back west ready to start the GRA training program at Evergreen. Huelo and I talked on the phone every night. I was sitting in class with Aimi when I told her that I couldn't stop thinking about Huelo and I might need her help. American Express had a travel program for students at the time. They offered two round trip tickets within the United States for $99 so long as you were a full-time student and had an American Express credit card. During a break I called American Express and booked a flight to NYC. That night I asked Huelo if she had received the package I had mailed several days earlier. She said that she had not. I told her that I missed her and hoped that it would get there in a day or two.

The next morning Aimi drove me to the airport. She and her roommate said this surprise cross country visit was the most romantic and daring thing they'd ever heard of anyone doing. I got on the plane and was seated next to a lady reading a novel. She politely asked where I was going, was it business or pleasure, the usual conversation starters. I told her that I had met this girl a few weeks ago and was on a surprise visit. "Wow" she said, then after a long awkward pause... "Well, good luck". Up until Aimi and this lady's responses I hadn't given the plan a second thought. This is what we in the business call a planning fallacy. It usually occurs when someone's intuition (that Huelo liked me and wanted to be with me) gets magnified by an over inflated ego. The balloon of over-confidence is then either deflated by doubt or popped by reality. I had a five hour flight to torture myself with "what if" scenarios that all ended up with a door being slammed in my face and me sleeping in some fleabag hotel.

The plane landed in New Jersey and I hopped on a train for NYC. Using a map I navigated my way to her neighborhood all the while an imaginary ulcer the size of a half dollar was eating through my duodenum. Should I stop and call her? It was an overcast day which I thought was good. I'd be a nice surprise on such a gloomy day. I got to her apartment complex and the person leaving was kind enough to hold the door open for me. It would have been a crushing defeat if I buzzed her apartment and was denied entrance to the building. It was a little after 5 pm. I climbed three flights of stairs to the big black door that separated absolute euphoria from ultimate humiliation. My heart was racing, my mind was racing, I took one last deep breath and knocked on the door.

Huelo opened the door and jumped into my arms starting to cry. Fortunately, these were tears of joy. No homeless shelter, hostel or fleabag hotel for me. We had a great two days before I had to go back west. Aimi picked me up from the airport. I was emotionally exhausted. As excited as she was about my adventure she was certain that I was going to get fired for skipping GRA training. After the GRA director blew off steam about my irresponsibility I informed her that the first two days of training were the same as the previous year's course. That I was already CPR certified and that she (Huelo) was worth it. She acquiesced and I remained a GRA.

The distance and our demanding schedules finally got the better of our relationship. Initially, if we were

going to have Friday, Saturday and Sunday together
the anticipation and adrenaline would maintain
euphoria until an hour or two before leaving for the
airport on Sunday. The post-partum depression and
black cloud of despair not only persisted for a few
days afterwards, but started infringing on our time
together. Nine months into the relationship we
decided it should end. The black cloud of despair
was casting too large a shadow. We are still best of
friends and smile when thinking about those crazy
coast to coast trips.

Maximillian's roommate, Wellington, was an
artificial intelligence genius. His first video game
resembled the Black Knight in Monty Python's Search
for the Holy Grail. Arms that got lopped off would
squirt blood five feet to the side. This was usually
followed by some irrational challenge to the other
combatant's manhood. It was so gory at the time it
was banned in the United States. That ban made it a
big hit in Europe. Wellington like Tony was invisible
for the first nine months of classes. He didn't even
bother staying in the dorms. His most recent
computer game was about to launch so he slept at his
office most nights.

Maximillian's first few conversations with
Wellington were about cars. Maximillian had $10,000
left from his student loans and both were in the
market for a new car. Maximillian had been doing a
great deal of research on the subject and
recommended the Ford Escort. Maximillian wanted
to buy one but could not afford it. Wellington had

been driving a Volkswagen Rabbit with a
personalized plate: "IAMWELL". Wellington asked,
"What if money were of no concern?" "Well, if
money were of no concern", Maximillian said "he
would get the Ford Escort with the leather upgrade".
Maximillian bought a Hyundai as it was much
cheaper (about $8,000 at the time). Hyundai was a
new Korean car company and we used to joke about
what lasted longer a Hyundai or a Monday? (Answer
at the time: Monday). Wellington pulled in with a red
Ferrari. It had tinted windows and leather seats.
Victory Wellington. The only thing missing was an
"IAMBETR" or "BETRNOW" license plate.

One night we were discussing our bucket lists.
Wellington, having excessive cash flow from several
successful computer game endeavors was way ahead
on his list. He was well traveled, been sky diving,
bungie jumping, helicopter skiing, owned a red
Ferrari (with leather seats), but hadn't run a
marathon, done Ironman Hawaii or won a Nobel
Prize. Wellington was not interested in winning a
Nobel Prize but running a marathon and doing
Ironman Hawaii seemed pretty cool. Maximillian

and I went sky diving and we all signed up for the Los Angeles Marathon.

Daniella, Maximillian's girlfriend at the time, met us in Los Angeles. She was an amateur photographer who immortalized us on film at several different course locations. It was unseasonably hot that day, 104°F. I went out too fast and pulled a hamstring. So when Daniella photographed me at mile 17 I was, "suffering like I'd never suffered before". More importantly, from a historic smack talk point of view, was the innocent photographic bystander. He was a Hispanic male in his mid-30's running without a shirt. He was probably 20 pounds overweight and had a few auxiliary nipples on the left. That LA Marathon would forever be known as my race with the three nippled Mexican. When showing the picture I would always say, "I'm the two nippled Mexican. And no, I'm not being arrested."

Wellington and Tony joined us for the Green Castle marathon. Tony and I drove up the Friday before the race so we could visit with Katrina. Wellington joined us Saturday evening. He had been working on another of his bucket list items: becoming a Black Belt in Karate. He showed up with bruised ribs and a black eye as he had gotten the crap kicked out of him in a Karate tournament earlier in the day. For all future races we had to make sure there weren't any nearby karate tournaments race week. When it came to racing, we didn't want to hear any excuses. Katrina was in pre-clinical hell so she skipped the marathon. She'd race with us after medical school when she actually had some free time to train.

Moral of the stories: Working on bucket list accomplishments, taking big emotional gambles, and having friends make life worth living.

Chapter 4
The Cream Team

We frequented a very famous ice cream parlor near Evergreen. Wellington proposed that they sponsor us as a racing team. While training for our first Ironman we could advertise 15-20 hours per week. In exchange, we got all the ice cream we could eat. Thus, the Cream Team was born. Training runs and rides now had some intensity. There was a 100 yard steep grade we'd race up on every training run. Maximillian always won the sprint. Occasionally, he would give us a 10-20 yard head start, let out a war cry then blow by us near the top. He once told Wellington that so long as they were both living breathing carbon life forms he'd never beat him up Quadburn Hill.

One Sunday morning we decided to go to Wellington's parents' home for some open water swim training. Our plan was to swim a mile up the canal into the bay. After a 10-15 minute break we'd swim back for a BBQ. Maximillian, Tony and I were trying out our wet suits as we had never swam in one before. Wellington was not only "too sexy for his shirt" he was too sexy for a wet suit. He fashioned a tight speedo which left little to the imagination.

The canal swim went well but when we reached the bay, the visibility deteriorated. The water was stagnant and felt strangely thick. The increased viscosity was due to the lack of a current and thousands of jellyfish. It was probably the fastest most terrifying 500 meter swim of our lives. Speedo Boy was the first out of the water as he was the first to realize what was going on and the most vulnerable to a really bad outcome. After the break we walked around the bay and jumped in the canal to swim back in the jellyfish free zone. Amazingly, no golden showers were required.

That evening Maximillian started another hysterically funny tradition at the BBQ called distract

and devour. Maximillian might ask you to pass him
the salt or direct your attention to something or
someone in the environment. When you looked away
he would steal some of your food. He might get a
spoonful of your ice cream, a chocolate chip cookie or
stuff half of your burrito down his pie hole but he
usually got something. Tony was especially
vulnerable to these deceptions and lost a scoop of ice
cream during the first raid. It got to the point where
you just couldn't trust Maximillian around food.
Once we were eating at an outdoor café and there was
a loud screech followed by the indisputable sound of
cars crashing. Tony flung his arms around his plate
guarding his food like a mother eagle protecting her
nest. We all laughed and Maximillian commented
that his ventriloquism lessons were finally paying off.

After an eternity of training (six or seven months)
the day had finally arrived. It was the inaugural
Grape Vine Triathlon. Maximillian's parents flew in
from the Big Apple. Wellington's parents picked
them up from the airport and the four of them headed
to the wine country. We were all having a great time
at dinner when we decided we would race not just for
glory or bragging rights, but for the Hammer. The
Hammer was an affectionate title given to the one
who "laid the hammer down" and won the race.

Maximillian's mom started laughing hysterically.
Once she gathered her composure she told us another
legendary hammer story. When Maximillian was
three or four years old they had gone to a hardware
store to actually buy a hammer. When she got to the

register to pay for it she noticed that little Max, maybe Maxathousand or Maxahundred back then, had disappeared back into the store. He then came running up and proudly proclaimed, "I made dukey, I made dukey!" When she asked where, he pointed to one of the display toilets. Proud, yet mortified, she verified that the package had been delivered, provided positive feedback by congratulating him and then left the store as quickly as she could. She couldn't remember if she even paid for the hammer.

All of the pre-race jocularity was just nervous energy seeking expression. The lack of organization for the Grape Vine Triathlon only escalated the anxiety. The race was a cluster from the beginning. The day before the race we had to rack our bikes in one transition area then put our running gear in a second transition area 50 miles away. Back then rack position was first come first serve. English translation: "Hey, I want this position so I'll just move this racer's stuff over there" (and not say anything to anybody)… And Mr. Cowardly Cheater, who really should have been on medication, would literally throw some of your stuff in one direction and the rest in the opposite direction. Guys who took racing way too seriously always racked their gear last to gain those unearned competitive advantages. Testosterone poisoned racers obtained the primo positions in transition and caused significant chaos and confusion for other racers looking for their displaced gear.

The Grape Vine Triathlon swim consisted of two 1.25 mile loops in the shallow Tomahawk River. Pre-race instructions were to just stand up if you got out of breath or too tired during the swim. The pro athletes got a 5 minute head start before the chaos of a mass start for the age groupers. In the Hawaii Ironman, the 1800 age group racers have the entire Pacific Ocean to spread out in. The Tomahawk River was, at most, 20 yards wide. Thank goodness there were only 200 age group racers that day. Maximillian was not a good swimmer by any stretch of the imagination so he wisely decided to start at the very back of the pack. As he was finishing his first lap the pros were finishing their second lap. The public address announcer was going crazy on the microphone: "Ladies and gentlemen, this is amazing, unbelievable, but an age group athlete is leading the swim. I can almost make out his number (every athlete had their race number marked on their swim cap)… Yes, yes, it's Maximillian Tomasini from New York. He's going to win the swim."

Swim exit volunteers rushed into the water to guide him out. The crowd started cheering. Maximillian stood up and visualized high stepping out of the water, blowing kisses to the crowd, and having a 30-45 minute lead over us. There were no timing chips in those days. He could have had a story for the ages. But his conscience got the better of him and he pushed the volunteers away. The pro swimmers caught up and zoomed by him into transition. Realizing that Maximillian's swim technique was not as good as the pros they kindly returned him to the river for his second lap.

Being the last one out of the drink had its advantages. The first advantage was that he didn't need to remember which row his bike was racked. The only bike left in transition had to be his. The second advantage was that if some idiot had moved his biking gear it would be easy to find. The third advantage was the potential to pass more people than anyone else in the race. Each racer passed was positive reinforcement and provided a few seconds of somewhat legal drafting. There were no changing tents at the Inaugural Grape Vine Triathlon. Athletes had to wrap themselves in towels while changing out of their swim gear and into their biking clothes. The Race Director had warned us that we would have to be wearing something at all times or be disqualified. He didn't appreciate us asking, "What if we wore a smile while changing?"

One by one, Maximillian picked off male and female racers that finished the swim before him. More importantly, he was making up time lost to Wellington and Tony Baloney. Half way through the bike Maximillian caught and passed Wellington. It would take another 25-30 miles for him to catch Tony. Maximillian's parents had agreed to provide him racer updates at the swim to bike transition, miles 20, 50 and 80 on the bike and every 5 miles during the run.

At the mile 50 update Maximillian was informed that the parental units were going to stop for lunch and asked if he'd like for them to bring him something. Well, of course, a roast beef sandwich and some fries would be splendid. The importance of race nutrition was in its infancy at the time. At lunch the parental units decided it would be more fun to go wine tasting then take lunch back to Maximillian. After all, they were on vacation and several great wineries were nearby. Maximillian got to mile marker 80 but there were no splits and no lunch. He was relegated to eating Oreo cookies and drinking Coca Cola like the rest of us non-supported racers.

At the swim to bike transition Maximillian was the only one who found his bike without any difficulty. At the bike to run transition none of us found our shoes where we had left them the night before. Today racers rack their bikes at assigned positions based on their race number. Professional racers get the primo slots in transition and they can bring their gear race morning whereas age-groupers have to rack their gear the day before. If someone got caught moving another racer's bike or gear today, they would get disqualified.

Liability was not such a big issue in the early days of triathlon. Streets were rarely blocked off or regulated by police. Racers would have to stop at all red lights both on the bike and the run or be disqualified. We all carried course maps as it was very easy to get lost. No smart phones, goggle maps or Siri to guide us around. Nowadays, signs, volunteers and/or law enforcement officers make sure everyone stays on course.

At mile 5 on the run the parental units started fabricating the data: "You're doing great, Wellington and Tony are 20-30 minutes behind. Here's some leftover Brie cheese sandwich." They missed the scheduled update at run mile 10. They pulled up beside him at mile 15: "you're doing great, they'll never catch you." Then sped off to another nearby winery.

Another missed update at run mile 20. At mile 24 the car pulled up beside Maximillian and his mom leaned out the window: "Remember how we said that Tony was way back there?" Maximillian: "Yes." Maximillian's mom: "Well, we misjudged the distance a little" (English translation: we lied). Maximillian: "So where is he?" Maximillian's mom "About 5 yards behind you." Maximillian looked over his shoulder and there was Tony Baloney with a big Cheshire cat smile on his face. Tony's legs looked fresh with a bounce in his step like he was on a Sunday morning stroll around the park. Maximillian knew he was in trouble as he had expended a great deal of energy on the bike. Tony conserved energy on the bike and was a great runner.

Maximillian and Tony were both consistent sub-3 hour marathon runners. During the Grape Vine Triathlon they ran 3:30 and 3:15 marathons, respectively. Maximillian sensing the upcoming testosterone poisoned sprint to the finish, tried to negotiate a compromise: "Tony, we could race it in but it would probably be the most painful two miles of our lives, might even kill both of us. How about if we take it easy and finish together?" Tony agreed stating that: "It would be an honor and privilege to finish together." One millisecond later Tony took off like a bat out of hell. Maximillian responded with every ounce of energy he had left. Smoke and flames were seen coming out of his shoes as they crossed the line together. They ran seven and eight minute miles the first 24 miles then sub sixes the last two. It was impressive.

Moral of the stories: The joy of an ice cream and the memory of finishing an Ironman triathlon are to be both guarded and savored.

Chapter 5
Lake Sunshine and the Oasis in the Desert

The crazy heart-pounding sprint to the finish intensified for Tony and Maximillian the following May at the Tidal Lake Triathlon. The last half mile of the run was a steep downhill into a finishing shoot packed with coeds. The triathlon was sponsored by the Oceanside University Physical Education Department as a college challenge. Many fraternity brothers and sorority sisters came to the event to support their racer friends and enjoy the festivities.

The cold water always made the swim wet suit legal. The swim start and finish were via a steep narrow boat ramp. Even when the race directors changed the mass start to age grouped wave starts, most swimmers reported getting pushed, kicked or slapped the first one- to two-hundred yards. After the wrestling match in frigid water racers got to warm their legs up by walking or running back up the steep boat ramp into transition.

Professional racers started at 8 AM followed by age group athletes in 5 minute increments. The last wave usually started around 9:30 AM. The bike course was challenging with several mountain climbs followed by white knuckle descents. By the time most racers got off the bike, the ambient temperature was in the mid- to upper 90s F. It was easy to get sunburned and dehydrated. The cooling effect of wind from either Mother Nature or that felt by riding 15-40 mph distorted the perception of one's internal body temperature. Most athletes were way behind on fluids after riding 56 hill challenging miles.

Regardless of the bike course's difficulty, most athletes enjoyed the run course. The Tidal Lake Triathlon run course was special. The run started with an uphill climb that most recreational athletes walked up. A few miles of paved roads then off into the wooded trails. Dirt pathways and rolling hills played havoc with one's tempo. Most racers were dehydrated and questioned their own intelligence for doing something so stupid. Then the mirage in the distance appears. It's the topless water stop at mile six and all the pain you've been dwelling on magically disappears. Total physical and mental rehydration, at least for a minute or two. It's the only water stop where all the guys walk through, drink two cups of fluids and say, "I can't thank you enough." The women triathletes were treated to a little eye candy as well. Some of the male student bodybuilders in Speedos would flex for them or hand them water.

After a few rolling hills runners pass through the camp grounds where more delightful distractions were available. Many of the female racers from the day before and their entourages were in bikinis soaking in the rays. I think that the male racers from the day before and their fraternity brothers were drinking beer and playing Frisbee. Before you know it you're running down the steep hill towards the lake and the finishing line. Literally thousands of people were there cheering you on. Given that most of them were young beautiful two X chromosomers, Tony and Maximillian had extra incentive to finish strong.

After the race we always stopped for dinner, smack talk and lots of laughter. Tony swore he'd never do that race again because it was so hard. He acknowledged all the beautiful athletic women, the great scenery and the physical challenge, but he much preferred leisurely bike rides up and down the coast. So when confronted the following year with: "I'll never do that race again!" Mr. Baloney said that he "had forgotten about the proclamation and was going to write it down so he wouldn't forget next year". He only did the race three or four more times thereafter. Never underestimate the power of peer pressure or hot chics.

Wellington also had a Tidal Lake Triathlon experience for the ages. In secret he had been dating a smoking hot Asian chic, thick black hair, a beautiful smile and crazy smart. We all wondered if she was a freshman or a sophomore in High School much less College. Wellington claimed that she was an undergraduate in the Artificial Intelligence class that

he was the Teaching Assistant. The age difference
was obvious, almost Oedipus Rexish. Maximillian,
Tony and I were all uncomfortably jealous. We
teased him saying that the reason she did not come to
the race the previous year was because she could not
get permission from her parents. At the traditional
dinner stop the conversation came to rating the water
stop six talent. Wellington acknowledged that several
volunteers had been topless then remarked, "But they
were all ugly." To which we all laughed and called
Wellington out for lying. Oddly enough, the Dollface
wasn't at the race the following year.

**Moral of the story: never underestimate
the power that beautiful women have to
make strong intelligent men do stupid
things.**

Chapter 6
Glenwood Creek

We had been sky diving, ran a handful of marathons, did several triathlons and only had a few near death experiences. Wellington proposed that we raise the stakes and climb Mount Everest. "Why not?" Maximillian countered "only 5-10 experienced mountain climbers die there every year." Tony had hiked to base camp at Mount Everest once but had to take Bumex (a strong diuretic) as he got high altitude pulmonary edema. He could barely breathe and had to abandon the climb. I had gotten high altitude sickness in the lowly Colorado Mountains several times during ski trips. Maximillian, being the great negotiator suggested we climb Mount Shasta instead. He wanted to research its difficulty and use it to actually get some climbing experience. He also wanted to avoid inadvertent bragging if some of his friends' mothers or grandmothers had also climbed Mount Shasta. Big Al, Tony and Wellington continued to climb mountains but the rest of us just used them for skiing.

The abandonment of Mount Everest only prompted Wellington to propose we go kayaking down the American River. Not that any of us had any kayaking experience aside from seeing an occasional Mountain Dew commercial on TV. Those mirror neurons, which translate seeing an activity into a belief that one can actually do the activity, can lead to some bad decisions. When we rented inflatable kayaks the shop owner suggested we go to Glenwood Creek to take a half day lesson. That would have been the wise, rational, mature thing to do. But when you're trying your best to kill each other no one wants to go to Glenwood Creeeeeek (said with both rows of teeth showing and wiggling hands dangling in front like you have bilateral wrist drops). Seeing this taunt, the shop owner knew there'd be no lessons. He did advise us to paddle as fast as we could through the rapids. Speed was not only the secret to skating on thin ice, it was the secret to get through the rapids.

One only need to paddle through a few class one or class two rapids to build up a total false sense of security. We lost all of our cell phones, one set of car keys, two wallets and 99% of our collective kayaking confidence after the first two sets of class four rapids. The class four rapids never snuck up on you. You knew they were coming because there would be crowds of people watching. And they got their show. Even when paddling as hard as you could, if you entered the rapids on a bad line, Mother Nature

would suck you backwards into the turbulence of a
waterfall.

    The "Meat Grinder" was one such class four rapid.
Three of us tried to paddle around the large rock in
the river's center. But the backflow of water pulled us
backwards like a tractor beam in a Star Trek movie.
As the tip of the kayak would rise, so would your
anxiety. The back of the kayak would slowly be
submerged. You would be furiously paddling but
eventually the arms would tire and the boat would
capsize backwards. You could hear the crowd
cheering as you entered nature's washing machine. A
washing machine with snow melt water so cold it
takes your breath away and rocks on three sides.

"Look, that's me" I said when we were viewing the professional photographs at the rental shop. Wellington asked: "How do you know that's you?" I was upside down in the rapids everything underwater except one foot pointing at the sky. It was the sock that identified the body. Should you be adventurous or foolish enough to go kayaking, always wear a helmet and a life preserver. They're called life preservers for a reason. And Lord knows how many rocks we banged our helmet covered skulls against.

The American River Kayaking trip was the last time coordinating an event was easy. Tony graduated and took a job in Silicon Valley building scanning electron microscopes. I took a Residency training spot in the Deep South. It took Wellington another year or two to finish his PhD. He joined Tony in the Silicon Valley but they rarely ever saw one another, damn workaholics. Maximillian finished Medical School and took a Residency position at New England Cancer.

Katrina was still at Royale and finally broke up with Tyson. She had been enjoying her new found

freedom and irresponsibility until Lexington came
into the picture. Her original plan was to finish
school at Royale then move to Seattle for a Residency
Training program. She had been invited to a party for
the graduating seniors when one of her friends
introduced Lexington. Katrina told her friend that he
was nice but not to give him her phone number if he
should ask. Three days later Lexington called and
asked her out. Being polite Katrina agreed to go to
dinner. She explained her situation to him as follows:
"I just got out of a long term relationship. I am
starting my fourth and final year at Royale. I plan to
move to Seattle next year. Four years at Royale was
enough." Lexington, already head over heels in love
with her, would jokingly claim that he heard forty
years not four. Two kids and twenty years later
they're half way there. Turns out that Katrina's friend
never gave Lexington her phone number. He looked
her up in the phone book and called her on a land
line. This was the 1980's after all. Cell phones and
the internet were in their infancy.

Aimi got married in Las Vegas then moved to
LALA-land. She became the film producer she
always wanted to be. Wellington and I surprised
everyone by wearing Elvis costumes to the wedding.
If only we could have parachuted in like Nicholas
Cage did in "Honeymoon in Vegas".

Moral of the stories: when testosterone poisoned men are having fun trying to kill each other, it's called male bonding.

Chapter 7
PEG Tubes and Mr. Uncomfortable

After graduation I moved south for Internship and Residency Training. Our Department Chairman was a Spine surgeon and heard that I was interested in Spine. The Chief was a mountain of a man, six foot six inches, 280 pounds. After a successful college football career he opted for Medical School instead of the National Football League (NFL). At the time he graduated doctors made a lot more money than athletes in the NFL. He looked after me like Chief Bromden looked after RP McMurphy in One Flew Over the Cookoo's Nest. He tailored my rotations to give me the best possible training to become an Orthopedic Spine Surgeon. Surgery Internships consisted of 12 one month rotations through the various surgical subspecialties: Vascular Surgery, Neurosurgery, General Surgery, Emergency Medicine, etc... More important than the rotation was the instructor and hospital at which the rotations occurred.

My first rotation was with Dr. Bienville on the Vascular Surgery service. Dr. Bienville was the undisputed best vascular surgeon in the region. He did all the anterior spine exposures for the Chief. He was also one the Chief's best friends. It was my first day as a real doctor. I could give orders, write prescriptions and make patient care decisions. We finished rounding on 15-20 inpatients and headed to the endoscopy lab. As a favor, Dr. Bienville was putting in a PEG tube into the Chief's mother. She had dysphagia and decided to stop eating. A PEG tube is rubber tube 10-12 mm in diameter that a surgeon places through the skin directly into a patient's stomach for nutritional support. The insertion technique involves passing an endoscope (5 mm in diameter flexible tube with a light and a camera at its tip) down the patient's throat into their stomach. Once the surgeon sees a light just below the rib cage on the left she rotates and pushes the light up against the abdominal wall. The illuminated spot signifies the surgical target and holds it in place. The surgeon then anesthetizes the skin and jabs a trocar (nail) into the stomach. The trocar's position is confirmed by the endoscopic camera. The sharp tip central portion of the trocar is removed leaving a hollow cannula in place. The PEG tube is then inserted through the hollowed cannula, the cannula is removed and the PEG tube anchored to the skin with sutures. I had seen one or two placed in Medical School (U-Tube hadn't been invented yet).

The patient was waiting for us in the lab. She was elderly, very thin and not very happy. Her image reminded me of World War II concentration camp victims. Dr. Bienville talked to her for a few minutes then explained the procedure. He instructed her to open her mouth wide. But when the endoscope touched the back of her throat she decided that that was far enough. Resistance involved either grabbing Dr. Bienville's arm or the endoscope. As the two of them were arm wrestling she gaged then coded. That is, her heart stopped beating and lungs quit breathing. Without batting an eye we started cardiopulmonary resuscitation (CPR) but to no avail. She was pronounced dead 45 minutes later. Dr. Bienville started crying and said: "Don't ever forget this: no matter how easy you think a procedure might be you can always screw it up and kill someone. Now I've got to go tell my best friend I just killed his mother."

Later that same night I was on call and received a consult from the Intensive Care Unit (ICU) to put in a central line. A central line is a large diameter catheter placed into either the subclavian or jugular vein. General Surgeons usually target the subclavian vein, behind the collarbone, as they are more familiar with chest anatomy. Anesthesiologists prefer jugular vein cannulation as it allows easier access for them during surgery. I was trained on the subclavian technique and was a General Surgery Intern so I trotted off to the ICU to place a subclavian. The procedure went well and the post-procedure X-ray showed the tip of the catheter in good position pointing downwards towards the heart rather than up towards the head. The lungs remained fully inflated. If you're overly aggressive during needle insertion you can puncture a lung and/or cause an excessive amount of bleeding into the chest. All was well so I went back to the call room to get some shut eye before morning rounds.

Next morning I showered, shaved and left for the conference room when I was blindsided by the third year General Surgery Resident: "What the hell were you doing putting in a central line? What would you have done if you dropped a lung? Why didn't you call me?" I responded: "Dude, I did three of these as a medical student and you're telling me that I have to wait three years before I'm "qualified" to place one as a doctor? I've also put in a few chest tubes but I imagine that's a fifth year General Surgery procedure?" That was my first day as a doctor. How in the world was I going to make it a week, much less a year, without getting fired?

Dr. Bienville's trust in my surgical skills increased daily. Once the critical part of the case was done he'd say, "Are you OK to close from here?" I'd respond "Absolutely." He would then break scrub and run to the bathroom in the male doctor's changing room and smoke a cigarette or two. Patients and physicians openly smoked in hospitals throughout the 1980s. The Veterans Administration (VA) Hospitals had cigarette girls for the GIs and doctors up until the 1990s. They would wear mini-skirts and high heels. The trays were supported by a leather strap over a shoulder. Too bad someone figured out that smoking was bad for one's health. Don't believe me? Watch the movie Rocky II. In the movie Adrienne is in the hospital after childbirth and Paulie is smoking a cigar in her hospital room.

After a month on the Vascular service I headed to the Emergency Department. General Surgery interns rotated there for the trauma experience. In addition to the ever active Late Night Knife and Gun Club, amazingly stupid things happened on a regular basis. For example, one night the ambulance pulls in with a guy "boarded". Boarded is a fancy medical term referring to a patient who is tightly secured to a stretcher with seat belts or 3 inch tape over the chest, abdomen, arms and legs. The neck would also be immobilized in a brace sandwiched between two hard foam pillows and secured with tape. Boarding patients prevented them from inadvertently paralyzing themselves, inflicting pain on health care providers and leaving against medical advice.

All boarded patients would be triaged over the phone, the (medically) unstable ones would go to Room 4. The call would go out over the loud speaker: "Room 4 in 2 minutes". The senior level Emergency Room (ER) Resident along with 6-8 Interns would congregate in Room 4 awaiting the patient's arrival. Occasionally the patient would be female but males had a monopoly on stupid and/or violent activities that would result in a trip to the ER. Each intern had an assignment for every patient that came in as a Room 4. One night you did the rectal exam checking for blood in the stool (usually present after a gunshot wound or stabbing to the abdomen). Other nights you took blood pressure readings or started intravenous lines. There was never a dull moment.

One night my job involved interviewing the patient and explaining what everyone was doing. Patients were much more likely to cooperate knowing that you're not just grabbing their junk and shoving a 6 mm silastic catheter into their pride and joy for shits and giggles. Foley catheters were used to determine if there was blood in the urine signifying injury to the kidneys or bladder. It was also comforting information that the doctor about to stick a gloved and hopefully well lubricated finger into your rectum was only checking for an injury to your colon. So I asked this guy: "Are you allergic to anything?" He looks at me smiling and says: "Yes, bullets." He must have been a repeat Room 4 offender to answer in such a calm, cool and collected manner. "What happened tonight?" I asked, thinking that he may have gotten shot. He had bilateral femur fractures.

It was very common for criminals in the Bayou region to just shoot victims in the thigh then steal their wallet. Those who protested got shot in both thighs. But this guy hadn't been shot. He was "helping a friend move," or so the story goes. They loaded up his friend's mattress and box springs in the truck bed but didn't have any rope to tie the load down. The patient told his friend that he would just ride in the back and hold the bed down. While they were driving through town at 25-30 mph everything was fine and the wind was refreshing. But when they got on the elevated expressway reality reared its sometimes ugly face. Mattress turbulence started when the car accelerated to 40-45 mph. Liftoff and the magic carpet ride occurred at 60 mph. He fell over ninety feet off the elevated expressway and did not stick the landing. That is, he did not land on the mattress. He was lucky to be alive. And before you ask, no, it was not an air mattress.

Once Aladdin was stabilized I headed back to the OB/Gyn cubicle. The rule was that any female coming to the ER with an OB/Gyn complaint got a complete exam, including Mr. Uncomfortable. Low and behold, a large woman complaining of discomfort in her female area was waiting for me. How large you ask? Large enough that I had to ask two other interns to assist with thigh retraction so that I could perform the speculum exam. While the three of us proceeded with the examination, she was hitting on me like there was no tomorrow: "Oh doctah, you got's the prettiest green eyes I'd ever seen." I'm like: "Didn't I see you check in with a 6 foot 3 inch 300 pound gorilla who could cave my head in with one swing of the fist?" To which she responded: "Oh he's just a snack, you da main course." All three of us got a good laugh out of that one. I then explained to her that since she was now one of my patients that it was against the law for us to get romantically involved.

Moral of the stories: things can go wrong in a blink of an eye, even pretty green ones.

Chapter 8
Sheiks, Dolphins and Camels

After the Emergency Room rotation I headed to the Neurosurgery service. Most Interns hated the Neurosurgery rotation, not me, I did it twice. The spine experience overlapped well with my intended profession and I liked the two Neurosurgery Residents on the team. The Fifth year Neurosurgery Resident worked as a late night disc jockey in college. If he didn't go into medicine, he could have been an excellent televangelist or greeter at Walmart. His humor, like mine, was way left of center. His December Internship rotation was in the ER. He had the other Interns string lights on him so he could be a Christmas tree in the waiting room.

One day we were rounding in the Neurosurgical ICU. Grace Hospital was built in the 1950s so there were no private rooms. All nine ICU patients on the ward had serious head injuries and donned white bandages (turbans) from their recent neurosurgical intervention. In bed one was a severe trauma survivor. In addition to the head trauma he sustained a broken arm, femur fracture and partial amputation of a foot. The radio in the Neurosurgical ICU only picked up one AM radio station. That morning a Warren Zevon song started playing. The former DJ and I started singing along. Then out of bed one: "Ahhhwoooh! Werewolves of London…" This guy had been in a coma for two weeks. He had numerous tattoos including lightning bolts in his pelvic region pointing to his "electric eel." We had been calling him Shazam for weeks because nobody knew his name but we all knew about the tattoos. When he finally recovered and was discharged from the hospital he asked, "Why was everyone calling me Shazam?" I told him it because he was a superhero.

Later that month I was helping the third year Resident perform a discectomy. Usually the Neurosurgeons could do this through a one inch incision but the female patient was a little on the large side. The three inch incision cut her dolphin tattoo directly in half. We discussed the case, the technique, the probability of a recurrent disk herniation and the tattoo. I was of the opinion that Flipper was a cover up tattoo. The Resident said lots of people had dolphin tats. The wound was closed and we went out to talk to the patient's mother and husband. After informing them that everything went well and that she should expect excellent pain relief we told them that we had one more question. Was the tattoo an original or a cover-up? As the husband's face turned red I realized what a terribly inappropriate question that could have been.

Fortunately, the mother started laughing and nudged him several times with her elbow. "Tell him, ha ha, tell him the story" she said almost goofy with laughter. "Why don't you tell him since you like telling the story so much" he said. Trying to compose herself she said: "OK. OK. So, it was his birthday (pointing at the husband). She secretly went out and got a tattoo. He got home early from work, so they went out for dinner and a movie. When they got home she went into the bedroom and lit a bunch of candles. He got undressed and hopped into bed. She hit play on the tape deck and some swanky strip tease music started playing. As she danced around the room she slowly disrobed. He sat up in the bed so he could enjoy the show. Once she got down to her undergarments she jumped on the bed. She was standing over him with one foot on either side when she finally took it all off. She then spun around 180 degrees, straddled him and shook her money maker right in his face. "What do you think?" she asked. "Who's Gary?" he answered. His name was Gerry. The ink master had misspelled his name or so the story goes. That was one birthday party they'd never forget. And that was the last time I ever asked about a cover up tattoo.

Two or three easy rotations later I was working in the Surgical ICU. The ICU Attending Physician assigned me the one orthopedic patient who was deathly ill. This guy had one foot in the grave and the other on a banana peel. I commented that he wouldn't die on my watch. Trying not to laugh out loud, the Attending smiled and complimented me on my optimism. I later realized that my optimism was really over-inflated ego disease rearing its ugly head (again). I knew the third year orthopedic Resident who assisted during the surgery. He did, and I was scheduled to do, a year of research between internship and first year of residency. Winston and I both enjoyed research and were planning on careers in Academic Orthopedics. Whereas I worked on 8-10

projects during my time in the lab, Winston finished
30. He was a machine working 16-20 hours a day
seven days a week. Winston emulated his namesake:
Winston Churchill. He was short, overweight,
balding and wickedly smart. Winston informed me
that the guy I was assigned to take care of was a Sheik
from the Middle East.

The Sheik had undergone bilateral knee
replacement and did not wake up after surgery. He
and 30 members of his extended family came to Gulf
Coast University two weeks before surgery so the
Sheik could be evaluated pre-operatively by the
cardiology, orthopedic, and anesthesia teams. While
the Sheik was being evaluated his family took day
trips: Las Vegas, Disneyland, Hollywood, Minnesota
(Mall of the Americas), etc… Apparently the Sheik
had rented Gulf Coast University Hospital's entire
top floor. His family used the floor as a hotel at the
bargain price of $50,000 per day. They could have
stayed at the Ritz for half the cost. So when the Sheik
didn't wake up after surgery, the eldest son was
rather upset. Winston said that the Orthopedic
Attending Physician, was using the back staircase and
visiting the Sheik at 5 AM. He was a little worried
that he might be the victim of some form of non-
recoverable non-accidental violence if the Sheik did
not experience a full and complete recovery. On post-
op day three I told Winston that I thought the Sheik
had turned the corner and "we were going to
extubate him today." Winston raised his hands above
his head and said "Praise Allah". It was funny

coming out of his mouth then and it is funny whenever it comes out of mine. I only say it every time something unexpectedly good happens.

Later that year I received an invitation from the eldest son to visit the Royal family in the Middle East. I flew there with my girlfriend and her 12 year-old daughter. For religious/political reasons we told them that we were married and Taylor was our daughter. After a week of traveling we were ready to head back home when one of the brothers approached me with a proposition. He explained that he and his brother found Taylor to be a very attractive young woman. They hoped that I would not be offended and offered to trade three camels for her. I promptly informed them that I was greatly offended as Taylor was worth at least six camels. They countered with a four camel offer. When I told them it was seven camels or nothing, the debate got heated. Voices were raised and after 30 minutes of "bargaining" neither side gave in, no agreement was reached.

It was a very quiet flight back to the states as my girlfriend was furious with me about the bargaining. Why in the world would I even consider trading Taylor for anything much less a few camels? Mid-flight Taylor leaned over and asked me if I really would have traded her for six camels. I assured her that I wouldn't have traded her as there was no way I could have fit six camels on the airplane. Bump, bump, bump... Another one (relationship) bites the dust.

Moral of the stories: always count your blessings (and your camels).

Chapter 9
Viagra and the Wellesley Effect

Research scientists are like rock and roll stars in only one respect. Neither the rock star nor the researcher knows beforehand which project will be their biggest achievement. Many times a mistake or joke will end up leading to something amazing. Take, for example, Maximillian's research team at Evergreen. They were testing a new anti-hypertensive drug. That is, a drug that was supposed to lower a patient's blood pressure thereby reducing the risks of strokes and heart attacks. One year into the clinical trial they discovered that men receiving the new drug were dying of heart attacks at a ratio of 20:1 compared to those men receiving the traditional anti-hypertensive medication. The stroke ratio was just as bad. They reported these adverse reactions to the Food and Drug Administration (FDA) knowing full well what the consequences would be: The FDA would shut down the trial immediately and the lead investigator would have a permanent failure on his record. Maximillian, being the lowest team member on the totem pole, was charged with notifying all patients that the trial was over. His highest priority was to inform the study patients of these newly identified dangers and request that all of the new anti-hypertensive medication be returned immediately. The female subjects in the trial and the men in the control arm of the trial gladly returned their samples as requested. The men receiving the high risk for heart attack drug refused to return their samples. Some said that their pet ate the medication, others said they had flushed it down the drain, and some told him that "unless someone was going to hold a gun to their head there was no way in hell they were giving those pills back." That's when Maximillian turned a potential black eye into a golden halo, and discovered the truth. It was assumed that the male patients were having heart attacks because their blood pressure was dropping too low (transient systemic hypotension). Their blood was dropping anatomically lower, not systemically. High blood pressure apparently makes Mr. Happiness go into hibernation. The new anti-hypertension medication woke up the sleeping giant or midget, depending upon the case. Those heart attacks in men receiving the study medication were from over exertion not under perfusion. Henceforth, all advertisements for erectile dysfunction medications instruct patients to "check with your physician to make sure your heart is healthy enough for sex…"

While Maximillian was busy discovering one of the biggest "recreational" drugs of the 20th century I was counting shadows on the wall. The titanium wear debris in total hip replacement failures gave me plenty of time to lip synch Milli Vanilli songs and exercise. Katrina, Tony and I all ran the Houston Marathon during my time in the lab. The course in Houston was pancake flat and at mile 19, a former United States President waived at all the runners as they passed his residence. The real challenges were the humidity and warmth. In addition to George, there was a mile stretch near Rice University were the street was lined with alternating American and Texas flags.

Those patriotic thoughts and feelings that occurred during the race might have primed some post-race decisions. What is more American than Fast Food? I'm usually a post-race DQ Blizzard kind of guy. But post-race cravings have taken me for pizza, burgers and to places that I hadn't eaten at since grade school. Why? Who knows? I've had friends take taxi cabs through the drive thru to get a cheeseburger. After the Houston Marathon Katrina and Tony Baloney wanted to go to the Golden Arches. Tony said he was so hungry he could eat a dozen hamburgers. The bet was on, eat 12 and Katrina would pick up the tab. Feeling rather confident, Tony ordered a side of fries with the first order of six burgers. At the 8 burgers mark Tony wanted to stop eating the pickles. Nope, that was not part of the deal. Twelve burgers, pickles and all or no deal. Tony got to burger number eleven and blew chunks. Fortunately for us and the other patrons, he caught all of them in his extra-large drink cup. After wiping off his bottom lip he finished off the last two burgers and claimed victory. Of course, the Russian judge would have disqualified him, but that wasn't part of the deal either.

Our Houston marathon times qualified us for the following year's Boston Marathon. As 95% of all Boston Marathon runners were time qualified, it's a fast and prestigious race. The other 5% were fundraising spots or spots auctioned off by the host to increase revenue. For safety reasons, non-time-qualified runners had to start at the back of the pack. A few racers take racing way too seriously and are often hostile when passing slower runners whether the slowness was due to injury or ability. In the Boston Marathon, a runner's qualifying time determined their race number and corral from which they started. Maximillian, Tony and I started in corral number 14 (of 26) Katrina was in corral 16. We were in a group of 1,000 runners who had qualified with a time between 2 hours and 50 minutes and 3 hours. The course in Boston was slightly downhill and well supported. The race was always on Patriot's Day, a holiday in the Boston area. Many people along the course route host Marathon parties to cheer on and/or harass the racers. The Yankees were usually in town playing the Red Sox at Fenway and if the Bruins were in the Stanley Cup Finals, the energy in Boston was crazy exciting.

The course route takes runners past Fenway and one Wellesley College. Wellesley is an all-girls college. On a sunny day the coeds are 5 deep wearing bikini tops and screaming their heads off. Of course, they're 10 deep and many were topless when you're telling your buddies who didn't qualify. Sometimes you even buy your buddies a shirt as a little reminder of what they missed.

Some people believe that the Wellesley Effect is the synchronization of menstrual cycles for roommates at Wellesley. I believe the Wellesley Effect is the ability of women to influence men to do stupid things. Case and point: during the marathon runners usually settle into a slightly faster than average pace within the first few miles. Ten miles into the marathon you're running along at a good clip, if you could keep that pace, you'd finish with a personal record (PR, as the Hammerheads call it). Your heart and respiratory rates are way above average. You are running with the fastest, most competitive, marathon runners in the world on one of the fastest courses in the world. Then the pace accelerates and you think, "What the hell is going on?" You realize that you're about to hit the Wall of Thunder (at Wellesley). If you're on the right side of the road it is a special moment. Some one X and one Y chromosomed idiots will drop and give them 20 (push-ups). Other XY chromosomed idiots take their shirts off and sprint the half mile. The remainder of the testosterone poisoned mass of stupidity just run a little faster than planned. That is what I call the Wellesley Effect. Whereas triathletes walked through the Tidal Lake Triathlon water stop 6 for emotional and physical rehydration, runners expended way too much energy passing the Wall of Thunder. The only other time the pace normally accelerated was during the last mile to the finish line.

Our second Boston Marathon was even more interesting. Maximillian graduated medical school, married Daniella and accepted an Internal Medicine Residency Position at the New England Cancer Institute. Joshua resigned his position in a Neurosurgery Residency Training program to take a vacated space in the Orthopedic Training Program at Cobalt. Firing Orthopedic Residents was pretty common in those days. Orthopedics offered a better lifestyle with fewer hours and healthier patients (broken bones vs. brain tumors). Accepting the position in Orthopedics also allowed Joshua to make several lifestyle decisions. Most importantly, the decision allowed him to pursue a new love interest.

Joshua left the Sugar Daddy for the taste a younger man. Federico was true eye candy, a prototypical pool boy. He had a ripped abdomen, golden brown skin, a cool South American accent and a burning desire to be a kept man. Federico actually seated Joshua and the Daddy for dinner one night and it was lust at first sight for Joshua. Joshua and Federico were soon a couple. New England now homed two

of my best friends, Joshua and Maximillian, which
made the Boston Marathon weekend even more fun.

Walking Eagle, a friend and wannabe distance
runner, wanted to see the race and join in the
festivities. The Yankees were playing the Red Sox
and he decided that we all had to go to the game.
Joshua went to the hospital to make rounds but
would be back by 10 AM. At 9 AM a knock at the
door and Federico got picked up by the INS. Yes,
Federico was an illegal alien. He came to the States to
escape persecution for being homosexual. Joshua had
already hired an expensive legal team to work on his
appeal for asylum. Federico was not planning on
going to the game and fortunately we were there to
inform Joshua when he got back. Joshua had to deal
with the legal ramifications of getting Federico
released but agreed to give us a lift to Fenway. We
were in Joshua's convertible about two blocks from
Fenway when the Walking Eagle hopped out of the
car while it was still moving. We had planned to
walk back to Joshua's place if no tickets were
available. Walking Eagle, a fast talking salesman, had
negotiated tickets for us before I even got out of the
car. At the time, New York and Boston were first and
second in the American League standings. It was a
holiday weekend and lots of alcohol was being
consumed. Extra security was at Fenway as there had
been fights in and around the stadium. In the sixth
inning Walking Eagle turned towards me and said,
"Hey, that's Paul O'Neil, he used to play with the
Cincinnati Reds. He's going to hit me a home run".

Now Jaybird's nickname was Walking Eagle for a reason. He had to walk because he was so full of shit he couldn't fly.

When Walking Eagle said that Paul was going to hit him a home run I assumed he meant just hit a home run in his honor, not actually hit a home run such that he would catch the ball. But sure enough, on a 2-1 pitch, the left handed hitter Paul O'Neil smacked a pitch into deep right field and it was coming directly towards us. Everyone stood up in excitement and anticipation. Five foot six inch Walking Eagle jumped up onto his seat reached up with both arms over his head and stretched out towards the ball. Then, smack! A sound just like the one when Paul O'Neil hit the ball pierced through the crowd and Jaybird went down. I was worried that he had a concussion or might even be dead. Everyone held their breath until he staggered to his feet. His glasses were crooked on his face and the left eye already swollen and blackened. The ball had obviously hit him in the face. As there had been many fights someone looking to start another demanded to know what happened. Walking Eagle in typical fashion said, "I saw the ball it was coming right to me and when I reached up and caught it someone grabbed my arm and threw me to the ground. I must have hit my head on the armrest because I would never have let that ball go. I don't remember much after that." The fans were now in a frenzy and someone yelled: "Who has the ball?" Immediately, the guy with the ball extended his arm

out to Walking Eagle and said, "Here, it's yours."
Cheers erupted from the crowd again. A week later I
was recounting the story to my accountant who lived
in Cincinnati. He said that he played tennis with
Peter, Paul's brother. I gave him the ball and he got
Paul to personalize it for the Walking Eagle. How
cool is that?

As for the marathon, Maximillian took a year off
competitive racing to focus on work and re-
impregnating Daniella. He agreed to meet me on
course at the half way point and "run me in" as a
Bandit. All the big races discouraged Bandits as they
clogged the road, consumed food and fluids, and
shifted the cost to those who had qualified and paid
for the pleasure of a 26.2 mile sufferathon. No matter
how hard the race directors tried Bandits always
joined the races. Bandits made fake bibs, wore timing
chips from other races or in Maximillian's case joined
in the middle and exited before the finish line.

Some Bandits served as mules (carrying fuel or
fluids for their friend), others were doing it for glory
(to tell their friends that they actually ran the race),
and some, like Maximillian were just pacing a friend.

There were several problems with this plan: (A) Maximillian was always the faster runner; (B) I had already run 13 miles before his fresh legs joined the race; (C) he was well hydrated when he joined in I was not; and, (D) he used all of these advantages to torture me for the next 13 miles. After several miles of begging and pleading he finally agreed to slow the pace until we got into town.

We were a mile or so from the finish line when the pace picked up (again). We turned left onto Boylston Street and were closing the gap on a female runner in front of us when I eased up. "What are you doing?" Maximillian asked incredulously, "you've got her"

(meaning I could easily pass her). I agreed but pointed out that something was drastically wrong.

It was very easy to get blistered during a marathon. If you forgot to Vaseline up, wore new shorts, or got dehydrated, your feet, toes, thighs, underarms and/or nipples could easy get rubbed so raw they'd bleed. If that happened, walking was going to be painful for the next few weeks. But this wasn't blister fluid or a female related monthly accident with bad planning. This was soilage. I had run enough races to know that when Mother Nature called, you answered. If you thought you could put her on hold or send her to voicemail, you were mistaken. Runner girl probably thought she could make it to the finish line or didn't want to stop at a port-a-potty so when the second call came in, Mother Nature cashed out. I learned that lesson a long time ago. After ignoring Mother Nature's first two calls an emergency squat in between two parked cars was required in the Chicago Marathon. Thereafter, whenever She called, I answered (waiting line or not) at the first port-a-let available. Think Harry in the famous explosive diarrhea scene in "Dumb and Dumber." Then imagine the smell and your appearance until you can get to your morning clothes bag. Those shorts either get thrown out immediately or burned, even though it wasn't their fault.

After pointing out this keen observation to Maximillian I informed him that there was no way in hell I was going to try to pass her. She was the better runner. She was ahead of me for at least 25 miles as neither of us could recall getting chic'd by her over the last 12 miles. I explained to Maximillian, "I'd pass her, she'd pass me then we'd cross the finish line at the same time. Finish Line photographs would then document me as the guy who runs marathons with three nippled Mexicans and women who crap on themselves." I happily finished 20 yards behind her thank you very much.

Soon after the Boston Marathon Walking Eagle did his first ever Marathon. I bought a white T-shirt and had all his friends sign it with good luck wishes. The best part of the gift was afterwards. Walking Eagle thanked me as hundreds of runners wished him well during the race as the shirt noted that he was a virgin marathoner. Shirts worn during a race can be a blessing or a curse. One of Maximillian's friends was running Boston after a successful fundraising campaign. He wore a police officer's shirt for the race. He had gained a few pounds since college and did not adequately prepare for the race. So when he started walking around mile 15, an ever so supportive beer drinking, stogie smoking fan eating a brat commented, "Guess you had a few too many donuts huh Blue?"

Moral of the stories: life is like a marathon, it requires a lot of hard work, it entails a lot of suffering, then you die.

Chapter 10
Child Beating, the Hedonic Treadmill and Steel Dicks

Tuesday mornings at Gulf Coast University started with Grand Rounds and Tuesday evenings concluded with fracture conference. Fracture conference involved the first year Residents gathering all the patients' X-rays that were treated for fractures during the previous week. X-rays were then placed on a view board while the first year provided patient demographics, injury description, fracture classification and possible treatment options. Cases were discussed one at a time. As instructed by faculty, the upper level Residents would then aggressively ask questions to test the first year's knowledge. I likened it to emotional child beating. If you were humiliated as a first year Resident and it "made you stronger" then you should emotionally berate the first year Residents when given the opportunity.

I've been informed that rats who received an electrical shock (painful stimulus) in the test box will often bite another rat of lower status when returned back into the general population of rats. Thus, the alleviation of self-pity by inflicting pain or asserting dominance over a less powerful member of society is an evolutionary feature common to rats and orthopedic residents at Gulf Coast University. The tradition of the senior level Residents tormenting the incoming class with total immunity persisted for decades. Thus fulfilling the adage that shit really does flow downhill. The harassment dissipated when the upper levels became distracted with employment interviews and Board Exams.

One of my classmates had a photographic memory. He scored at the 99th percentile on every standardized test he ever took. When we were Interns he was forbidden from taking the General Surgery In-Service Exam. The General Surgery Chairmen across the country usually required all Interns to take the exam in order to lower the national average. Theoretically this would make it easier for the seniors to obtain a passing grade. Teflon's one score could not raise the average but it would save the Chairman embarrassment of having an Intern score higher than the people who had been in his program for seven or more years. It would also preserve the dignity of the upper level General Surgery Residents who he might outscore.

It was Teflon's first (and last) day in the barrel at Fracture Conference. He presented a distal radius fracture and the upper levels questioned him on the classification system. Teflon gave them a history lesson on the four different classification systems, how they evolved, who the proponents of the systems were and how the two competing recommendations from Rockwood and Green Textbook of Fractures and Green's Hand Textbook differed. After citing textbook page numbers like the Rain Man, he was never pimped again.

Gomez, on the other hand, had a bullseye on his back. As attacks on Teflon's fund of knowledge subsided, the upper-level bullies redirected their aggression towards Gomez. He used to get so nervous he'd throw up minutes before his Grand Rounds presentations. Grand Rounds was an hour long conference during which one Resident gave an in depth 45 minute presentation about one particular topic. The Residents who spent a year in the lab had the advantage during Grand Rounds. We had 10-12 prefabricated talks. All we had to do was review the slides before the presentation. Gomez and the others had to start from scratch. They would have to find a representative case with X-rays then do the research review.

Grand Rounds never bothered me. I was planning on going into Academics so public speaking was just part of the deal. During my research year the Chief asked me to put together a Grand Rounds presentation on: Complications Associated with Multilevel Cervical Spondylolysis. He wanted to go to the Pain in the Neck Society's Annual Meeting in Santa Fe, New Mexico. The abstract was weak but The Chief was a former Society President. He got to go to one of his favorite venues and I added a line on my Curriculum Vitae.

The beatings one took in Grand Rounds were nothing compared to the abuse dished out at the Pain in the Neck Society meetings. Grand Rounds at Gulf Coast University might be attended by one staff member having some expertise on the chosen topic. But if that expert didn't show up rarely would anyone else have any cutting insights to embarrass you with in front of your colleagues. At the Pain in the Neck Society meetings there were hundreds of world experts anxious to dish out jaw dropping personal and professional insults at the drop of a hat. Sometimes the rats were biting other rats perceived to be lower on the academic ladder. Other times it was calculated aggression challenging the dominant animal (expert). Each session had three five minute presentations followed by 20 minutes of "discussion". Discussion was a polite way of indicating the time reserved for audience insults, reprimands and humiliations. Remarks were often tainted with an undertone of aristocratic snobbery. A famous barb came when a moderator once commented, "That might be how cervical fusions look in La Jolla, but that's not how they look in Bradbury."

Having witnessed these public lynching I was a bit worried. Not since I had to knock on Huelo's door had I experienced such anxiety. My presentation reviewed a surgical technique with an exceptionally high complication rate. My suggestions to reduce possible complications might generate offense or audible laughter from the attendees. Fortunately, there was a Neurosurgeon who presented recommendations to keep patients intubated (on the breathing machine with a tube down their throat) in the ICU for 7-10 days after multilevel cervical fusion surgeries. This recommendation raised a lot of eyebrows as most patients were extubated and breathing spontaneously within an hour of the surgery's end. I could feel the unrest in the audience as many surgeons started loosening up their arms like a relief baseball pitcher in the bull pen. By the time my presentation was finished they were 10 deep at the microphones. For the next 20 minutes beautifully polished stones whizzed by my ears and pummeled the fellow presenter with pinpoint accuracy. I didn't need to interview five people in Academics to realize that the social hierarchy in Academic Orthopedics was established in a manner similar to that which gorillas use: aggression.

Fortunately, not all conferences were that malignant. I once presented at a very enjoyable conference in Big Sky, Montana. The conference was held at a World Class Ski Resort. As I forgot to pack ski gloves, I meandered over to the ski shop with my eye candy, the Sweet Thang. I grabbed the first pair of gloves I could find and headed towards the cashier. The Sweet Thang was trying on a white ski jacket with black trim. I was not sure what was wrong with her current (new) ski jacket but it was obvious she liked this one too. I offered to buy it as a gift but she politely declined. That night cognitive dissonance got the best of her as she was still actively running on the hedonic treadmill. She went back to the ski shop the next morning and when another Dos Ecquis (individual with two X chromosomes) was trying the jacket on, she knew she had to have it. As soon as the jacket was back on the rack she swooped in and bought it. As we headed out to the ski slopes a third Dos Ecquis wearing the same white jacket with black trim was walking directly towards us. I knew better to say anything as the steam coming out of Sweet Thang's ears was melting the nearby snow pack.

Like most Y chromosome skiers I'd been skiing in the same outrageous multi-colored jump suit for the past 20 years. I bought it in college, projected it onto card 16 of the Rorschach, and wore it ever since. In 20 years I'd never seen another skier wear a similar outfit, until that day. He was snow boarding down a run and as I passed him I yelled, "Nice suit dude." He caught up to me and we rode the chair lift up together and did a few runs. He too had never seen, much less met, anyone with the same ski suit. Naturally, I invited him to dinner that night and we had a grand time. Turns out he was a Veterinarian Spine Surgeon from England presenting at a conference the following week. That's the difference between the XX and the XY chromosomers, at least when it comes to ski fashion and making friends.

Maximillian and Wellington joined us that weekend for some skiing. While on the chair lift we updated each other on our projects. The Internet was up and walking and Wellington had another idea. He argued that Internet chat rooms were a terrible way to meet a potential love interest. Chat rooms and e-mail allowed one lots of time to fabricate responses. These responses were often tailored to what the person thought the other person wanted to hear or, in many cases, blatant lies. Wellington wanted to create a web site where two people could be on the Internet together and "go on a date." His premise was that if you were on a date spontaneous things would happen that would be much more revealing of your personality than anything that could happen in a chat room or during a long time delayed exchange of e-mails. For example he said: "Imagine that your avatar and your love interest's avatar go on a ski date in Colorado. During the date a bunny hops across the trail. It would tell your date one thing if you purchased a camera from the web site to take a picture of the rabbit. It would tell your date something very different if you bought a gun and shot it."

My skepticism about the internet dating site being one of the dumbest ideas I'd ever heard lasted for almost two years. I was in Silicon Valley and paid Wellington a visit. He had raised $50M in venture capital to build the web site. We were walking down coffee shop row discussing the project when we ran into one of his acquaintances. Mr. Egomaniac worked at Digital Sports Incorporated (DSI), the leader in the video game industry. The conversation went something like this: Egomaniac: "Well, well, Wellington, what are you doing these days?" Wellington: "Just hired my 40th employee to build a new virtual reality web site for dating." Egomaniac: "That's great. We still have room for you at DSI. You can run the soccer or ping pong division. Both have teams of 60." Wellington: "No thanks, I've tried the corporate life before and it wasn't a good fit." I was standing next to Wellington completely ignored. Wellington did not introduce me and Mr. Egomaniac did not even acknowledge my existence. I wasn't invisible, I was truly insignificant.

After the egomaniac left I said to Wellington: "I wasn't a communications major in college but I did date one in college. Could you reinterpret the conversation for me?" Wellington explained that when the DSI executive said: "Well, well, Wellington, what are you doing these days?" He really meant: "Oh its Wellington the Entrepreneur (voice filled with sarcasm and imaginary eyes rolling in the back of his head). What meaningless and boring project are you working on now?" My response of: "Just hired my 40th employee to build a new virtual reality site for dating" was a jab at him saying, "At least my ideas are worthy of venture capital funding. The company was successfully growing as evidenced by the need to hire 40 full-time engineers. I don't have projects given to me by someone sitting in a Board room." The Egomaniac's response of: "That's great" was total sarcasm. The "We still have room for you at DSI. You can run the soccer or ping pong division. Both

have teams of 60" comment was saying that they had
divisions at DSI larger than my entire company. My:
"No thanks, I've tried the corporate life before and it
wasn't a good fit" translated to: "No thanks, I have
tried kissing the corporate ass and did not enjoy it.
You're much better suited for that line of work."

Like Wellington, I hated kissing the corporate ass.
I hated the gorillas and the rats who poisoned the
society of rational animals. I too wanted to transcend
my profession as an entrepreneur. One of the best
conferences about entrepreneurship I ever attended
was at Gulf Coast University. We were a short drive
to New Orleans so we had no trouble recruiting
world experts to give talks. Dr. Richard Steele came
down and delivered a very insightful talk on the
creative process. He explained how he had
repeatedly gotten into trouble during his training.
How could anyone with a name like Dick Steele ever
get into trouble? One time he was sent to the
Pathology department to do autopsies as punishment.
He noticed that at the level of the odontoid process,
the spinal cord, the odontoid and the cerebral spinal
fluid each occupied one-third the area of the spinal
canal. One publication later and it became known as
Steele's Rule of Thirds. He also explained how the
Steele osteotomy of the pelvis was discovered. Hip
osteotomies in children reduce the risk for hip
dislocation and make walking much easier. The
underlying problem is that the orientation of the
acetabulum is too vertical. The horizontal redirection
of the acetabulum is accomplished by breaking the

pelvis in one or two areas then bending the bone through an open growth plate or two in another area. Once the femoral head is "covered" the risk for dislocation is reduced. One day Mr. Oh-so-cocky Dr. Steele had made his two cuts but the acetabulum didn't budge (all three of the patient's pelvic growth plates had already fused). So he did what every desperate authority figure does in the presence of students, he improvised to save face. He made a third osteotomy in the pelvis. He was then able to move the acetabulum wherever he wanted. Once the femoral head was covered, he used screws to hold the pelvis in place until it healed. One more publication and this technique became known as the Steele Osteotomy.

I admired Dr. Steele, his hardships led great discoveries. Although I often wondered how he would have fared as an Urologist. I too spent plenty of time in the penalty box. I could clearly see, in full technicolor, that my humor wasn't always appreciated. My first patent was for a Dog Dish Toilet Bowl. I noticed that, much to the annoyance of dog owners, dogs liked to drink out of the toilet. I thought that I might capitalize on this phenomenon by creating a feeding and watering device specifically for the Fidos of the world. The bowl would be filled with water and the tank filled with food. My first Trademark application was for the phrase: "Wide Load Ahead". As you have seen similar phrases while driving on the freeway, the application was denied. Eighteen wheelers and oversized trucks use the politically correct warning: "Oversized Load". I wanted "Wide Load Ahead" for marathon runners like me, with large back ends. Running shorts adorned with this phrase provided warning to the runners about to make a pass and shamed those who just got passed.

Moral of the stories: humans have a lot more in common with lower life forms than we'd like to admit — even when our jackets don't match.

Chapter 11

The Prisoner's Dilemma and Pink Piñatas

While I was swimming in a sea of opportunities, Joshua was sinking in an ocean of bad decisions. After finishing the Residency program at Cobalt he wanted to do a Spine Fellowship. We had an opening at Gulf Coast University and based on my recommendation the Chief hired him. I was a senior Resident at the time and scheduled to do the Spine Fellowship the following year. Joshua was happy to hang out but the cumulative stresses were wearing him out. The break up with the Sugar Daddy was easy for him but hard on the Sugar. Dr. Daddy was distraught, emotionally volatile and unforgiving. Immediately after the break up he'd show up outside Joshua's classes crying and begging him to get back together. Other days he'd be mad and hateful, screaming obscenities at him and cursing his wretchedness. When the Sugar Daddy finally accepted that the relationship was over he requested that Joshua pay him back for the 10+ years of living and tuition expenses. Joshua agreed as the request was fair and reasonable. Joshua truly believed that the repayment would allow the Sugar Daddy financial, emotional and social closure on that chapter of his life. Under traditional Sugar Daddy laws, Sugar Daddies paid for all their Sugar Baby's living expenses: food, clothing, housing, tuition, travel and extravagances. So when the Sugar Daddy returned three weeks later with a "repayment contract" Joshua

signed it and gave it back without even reading it.
Note to reader: NEVER EVER sign a contract without
reading it or having your attorney read it, especially
when it comes from an emotionally unstable jilted ex-
lover.

Sugar's attorney wrote a contract in which Joshua
would repay him for 100% of all Joshua's living
expenses during their ten year relationship plus 50%
of all future earnings. Sugar reasoned that Joshua's
re-education expenses were an investment and that
he was entitled to the royalties. Joshua was naturally
upset when the first bill arrived and he finally read
the contract. In psychology we call the phenomenon
of being mad at someone else when in reality it was
your own fault, displacement. Joshua made the
mistake of not reading the contract. Joshua was the
one to blame. Instead of taking responsibility for his
error in judgement, Joshua got mad and displaced the
blame onto the former Sugar Daddy. Joshua
lawyered up and another expensive legal battle
commenced. Six figures later the Judge ruled that this
was not a matter of divorce. Joshua and the Sugar
Daddy had not been married (legally or otherwise)
and there were not any "common law" marriage
guidelines for gay couples living together for
extended periods of time. Instead, the Judge ruled
that this agreement was a legally binding contract
between two individuals in the Commonwealth.
Joshua entered into the contract of his own free will
and now was accountable to the terms and conditions
disclosed thereunder. The Sugar Daddy's legal fees,

Sugar Daddy's repayment expenses, Federico's legal fees for asylum, Federico's sugar baby expenses, and the costs of living in an expensive city kept Joshua continuously broke.

Joshua's financial struggles were a constant source of frustration in his relationship with Federico. Federico's entitlement mentality made him feel neglected when he couldn't attend lavish parties, eat at expensive restaurants or travel. Things that other Sugar babies did with reckless financial irresponsibility. Federico became distant and often threatened to leave. The Spine Fellowship at Gulf Coast University was supposed to give Joshua some time to clear his head and Federico time to appreciate their relationship. Then the event that would change all our lives forever happened. Federico came down for a visit. Joshua "found" a birth certificate that was age appropriate for Federico. The only problem was the name on the birth certificate: William Robert Johnson. Most South American pool boys weren't named Billy Bob Johnson.

Joshua was not only desperate to keep Federico in the States but also under his thumb. Impatient with the legal system and always low on cash he had an idea. He convinced Federico that all they had to do to get him a new identity was fool one government agent. Their story believably started with the claim that they went to New Orleans for a celebratory weekend. They were having a great time and got overserved in the French Quarter (believable). They left the bar after midnight and got mugged (again very believable). The muggers took William's passport and money (still very believable). William's mother mailed them a copy of his birth certificate. Joshua would claim that he knew William since grade school. Nine years familiarity was the government requirement. Federico would become William Robert Johnson after the new passport was issued. The new identity would eliminate attorney fees for asylum. Even better, Federico could "legally" get a job and pay for some of his own extravagances.

They rehearsed the story again and again then headed to the passport office. Cameron, the government official, gave them the required paperwork. Joshua and Federico filled out the paperwork and whipped out the Billy Bob birth certificate. Cameron had been making small talk with Joshua the entire time. She looked over the paperwork and proclaimed that everything appeared to be in order. Cameron then instructed "Mr. Johnson" to: "Raise your right hand and affirm that you William Robert Johnson swear to tell the truth, the whole truth and nothing but the truth so help you God?" Joshua heard the proclamation and didn't give it a second thought. Federico, on the other hand, heard "Do you (think you're fooling me with this Billy Bob fake birth certificate) William Robert Johnson swear to tell the truth, the whole truth and nothing but the truth (or you're going to burn in hell forever)?" Inside Federico's brain the room went black and a single overhead heat lamp used to interrogate prisoners was suddenly radiating hot light on him and him alone. The room temperature went up 30 degrees. Sweat was pouring down Federico's forehead. Then, over a load speaker, Cameron commanded "so help you GODDDDDDD!" With the reference to the Almighty echoing in his ears, Federico froze.

After a long pause, Cameron noticed Federico's blank stare and asked: "Mr. Johnson are you ok?" Joshua bumped Federico with his elbow: "William, Cameron is asking you a question. Are you ok?" Federico clawing his way of out of catatonia turned his head slowly towards Joshua and said: "I can't do this." Cameron immediately separated the two. With Federico in one room and Joshua in another, the Prisoner's Dilemma ensued. The Prisoner's Dilemma is a contrived experimental condition used to study cooperation and power. Two study participants, usually broke college students, are told that they and the other study participant were arrested after just having robbed a bank. The study participants are then separated. If prisoner #1 testified against prisoner #2 and the prisoner #2 remained silent, prisoner #2 convicted of robbery. He would be sentenced to 10 years in prison while the loose lipped prisoner #1 would walk out Scott free. If both prisoners denied any involvement (not ratting out the other), the police would convict them on the lesser charge that would result in both serving two year prison sentences. If both prisoners squealed, they would both go to prison for 5 years.

Joshua could have lied by saying that Federico had been living under the Johnson alias all along. He could have claimed that Federico fabricated the birth certificate and he was an innocent confederate. The likelihood of both of them spontaneously fabricating that story was minimal. Besides, if Federico shouldered any the responsibility for the crime, his deportation likelihood would increase almost as much as his asylum likelihood would decrease. If Joshua told the truth and Federico told them that Joshua forced him into this, Federico might walk out unscathed while Joshua would face numerous criminal charges. If both told the truth, they would receive lesser penalties than if one lied.

Joshua ended up with a felony conviction on his record for falsifying information on a government document. Federico later explained that he was OK with lying to Cameron and assuming a fake identity, but he couldn't "lie in the eyes of God." When reapplying for privileges a year later, in the community of professional child beaters, Joshua had to check the "Yes, I've been convicted of a felony since I last applied for privileges at ABC hospital in New England". Joshua had been "stealing" cases from the Establishment at Cobalt since returning from his Spine Fellowship. The felony conviction was the first bit of political leverage in the moral majority's battle to remove him as competition. The moral majority weren't interested in giving Joshua a negative reinforcement shock, like a rat in a Skinner Box. They were going to protect their territory like gorillas in the wild, with aggressive elimination of the competition.

Spine surgery has always been a difficult undertaking. Even cowardly surgeons doing easy single level spine cases have a 5% complication rate. If you're doing adult deformity you could be a world expert and struggle to maintain a 50% complication rate. If you were a spineless AdminisTraitor part of a corrupt establishment, or if you had a grudge against a Spine surgeon, all you had to do was wait. Complications always occurred. An AdminisTraitor could easily reclassify a complication from routine to "unexpected or unacceptable". Or, he could enlist rival spine surgeons to testify to safety committees that the surgeon in question was "not qualified to be doing such cases" or that he "had a long history of exercising bad surgical judgment."

Many spine deformity surgeries can last 10-12 hours. Most humans use the bathroom once or twice in a twelve hour period. That is, unless you're a jilted female astronaut driving across country to kill a two-timing currently married ex-boyfriend who shoplifted the pootang. Under those circumstances it's ok to self-catheterize to urinate into a bottle or wear a diaper. Most Americans also eat or drink something at least once every 12 hours. If you're the Hospital's favorite son, breaking scrub in the middle of a case to go to the bathroom, ingest some nutrition, or maybe have a foot massage was perfectly acceptable. If you were on the black list the mere act of leaving the Operating Room (OR) in the middle of the case could be classified as patient abandonment. Joshua should have known these political policies. Laws are passed by politicians and enforced politically.

As the story goes, another surgeon came into the OR to say hello. Joshua asked the other surgeon if he wouldn't mind standing in while he took a break (to deposit his paycheck, use the bathroom, and maybe grab a bite to eat). As soon as Joshua left the room, a gas passing rat squealed to the Hospital AdminisTraitor. The AdminisTraitor scurried down to the Surgery front desk. When Joshua returned 20 minutes later he was instructed to finish the case and informed that his hospital privileges were suspended thereafter. With a recent felony conviction, charges of patient abandonment, and a gaggle of hostile competitors fighting over one another to testify against him, Joshua might as well have flushed his medical degree and the 14 years of post-graduate education and training down the toilet.

Joshua's financial obligations were now overwhelming. In addition to the Federico's lavish lifestyle, Joshua now had five sets of attorney fees. Joshua had fees for his divorce from the Sugar Daddy, immigration fees for Federico, fees for the New Orleans debacle, fees to defend his medical license and fees his malpractice insurance would not cover. Perceiving no other legal avenues, Joshua explored the illegal avenues for financial gain. Some theorized that Joshua had well established ties with organized crime and left the OR that day to consummate a drug deal. Hold that thought as I have to tell you my story in parallel space time.

I had been thinking of ways to improve surgery ever since I gave that Complications of Multilevel Cervical Spondylosis talk in Santa Fe. Most of the problems were due to the crappy medical devices currently available. Spine surgeons used one of three cylindrical mesh cage designs. One pipe had triangle punches, one round holes and one had quadrilateral air spaces. With no engineering or design training I thought, "I could build a better device than those. After all, I had cut a beautiful woman's hair for three years without ever going to beautician school." So down to Home Depot I went to buy ¼ inch strips of wood and duct tape. Sweet Thang's Cervical Cage (STCC) was designed, patents were submitted and the long tedious pathway through the Food and Drug Administration (FDA) approval process commenced. I designed the STCC with numerous safety features to help reduce intra- and post-operative complications. After several iterations and biomechanical testing we applied for 510(k) approval from the FDA. In the 510(k) approval process one submits destructive testing data of their device and two other devices used for the indicated surgery. If your device has favorable biomechanical test data and no serious clinical issues had been reported with the comparison devices already in use, you're approved. The problem at that time was that there were exactly zero FDA approved cervical vertebral body replacement devices on the market. We therefore had to build it strong enough to withstand loads normally seen in the lumbar spine. We would then submit clinical follow-up data from patients that received the device for cervical fusions and ask the FDA for a cervical indication.

After receiving 510(k) approval for the STCC I started shopping it to the major spine companies. I visited Zimmer, Medtronic, and few others. One day I received a Federal Express envelop forwarded from my Fellowship Training Program. The package was from Boston and the letter inside provided a phone number and requested that I call to confirm or release my hotel reservation. I was excited because the Depuy-Acromed Headquarters was in Raynham, Massachusetts so I called the number. Did I dial the wrong number? I would swear the person answering the phone said "Fifth precinct." Then a deep voice then said: "Hello Dr. Hammer I'm Detective Charles Thomas. Can you tell me where you were Saturday night June 2nd?" I answered, "Yes, I was in OR 6 from 4 pm until 2 or 3 AM doing cases. I was on call and there was lots of trauma." The Detective then said, "I'm sure you have the appropriate documentation. The minute I heard your voice I knew you weren't the guy." Dejectedly I said, "I only have two friends in the New England area. One is never in trouble, the other has fallen on bad times." The Detective asked the identity of the hard timer. "Joshua Marks" I responded "and what did you mean by knowing that I wasn't the one?" The Detective then informed me that they had been following

Joshua for several months. They had wire taps and Joshua's contact person had a completely different voice profile. Joshua had been under investigation for drug trafficking for quite some time. On the night in question twenty pounds of methamphetamines inside a pink piñata, the shape of a penis, were delivered to the hotel front desk. When Joshua went to the front desk and picked up the package on behalf of Dr. Hammer, the police busted him.

Not only was Joshua trafficking drugs he was partaking in them as well. Drug use was a recurring bad habit and explained a lot of other bad decisions in his life. Drug use flunked him out of college as an undergraduate and disqualified him from the practice of medicine as a doctor. Looking back, his comment about us being there for the Boston Marathon when Federico got picked up by the INS now made sense. Joshua said that had we not been there when the INS came by that he would have assumed that Federico was at a two or three day Rave (a dance party at which large quantities of recreational drugs were consumed). Joshua probably accompanied Federico whenever possible. Maybe Joshua (and Federico) had been supplying their friends and party goers for years. Instead of reservations at a gay bar, Joshua's next ten years were spent in the gray barred hotel. His medical degree became truly worthless. When Joshua was paroled the Medical Board said he could be reinstated but would have to repeat a Residency and he would never be allowed to prescribe narcotics again. How many Residency Program Directors in

their right mind would accept a two time convicted
felon fresh out of prison into their training program?
Exactly zero, end of story.

**Moral of the story: if you find yourself in a
deep hole, stop digging.**

Chapter 12
Precordial Thumps, Brain Damage and Club 300

It was Christmas Eve and I was dead tired. I just got off call and had been up for almost 30 hours straight. I picked up our youngest daughter from day care and headed to the airport. Sweet Thang was already at her sister's house with our oldest child. Angela was still a baby and always enjoyed sleeping on my chest. We boarded the plane and both fell asleep instantly. I don't remember any emergency instructions, taxi, or take off. The next conscious event was hearing the Captain making an announcement: "If there is a doctor on board please press your call light." In a haze I reached up and pressed the call light. The stewardess came to my row and asked if I was a doctor? "Yes, what's wrong?" I asked. She leaned forward and whispered, "There is a passenger in the back of the plane that we are concerned about. Could you take a look?" I stood up and handed Angela off to the other stewardess.

As I stumbled down the aisle the stewardess explained that the passenger sitting next to the one in question called for help. He said hello to the passenger in question when they first sat down. The plane took off and both drifted off to sleep. The guy in the middle seat woke up and had to use the restroom. He noticed the big guy in the aisle seat wasn't snoring anymore. He wasn't breathing and wasn't responding to requests to allow for passage into the aisle. As we headed back to the passenger in question the overhead lights were turned on. The passengers who were asleep were now wide awake thanks to the Captain's request and the cabin lights. I got back to row 37 and there's this big fat guy dead as a doornail. He was probably five foot eight inches tall and weighed one biscuit shy of 300 pounds. He dressed middle class, dress shirt, bad tie and a big pot belly. His lips were purple, no radial pulse, no carotid pulse and he was not moving air (breathing) or responding to questions. I suggested we lay him in the aisle as it's really hard to do Cardiopulmonary Resuscitation (CPR) on anyone sitting upright in a chair. We started to maneuver him into the aisle when I lost my grip and the body crashed to the floor. His head hit the floor and the hollow coconut sound echoed throughout the plane.

The stewardess then handed me a plastic stethoscope like one you'd give your grandkid on her third birthday. Acting very doctorly-like, I placed the bell of the stethoscope on several areas of his chest. I looked upward and quenched my eyebrows trying to give the impression that I was concentrating. I then looked at the stewardess, shrugged my shoulders, held my hands palms up as if to indicate there was little doubt (that he was dead and question as to what she wanted me to do next). I told her that I couldn't hear a thing. I was referring to the passenger being dead, and the toy stethoscope with poor acoustics. She thought my hearing was impaired by the noise and commotion coming from the other 200 passengers. So she stood up, turned around, arms at her side, elbows locked straight, clenched her fists, took a deep breath, and screamed: "The doctor demands that you be quiet!" Oh snap, I thought, what am I going to do now? Guess I'm going to have to start CPR but I really didn't want to suck face with this dead guy. I have, however, always wanted to try a precordial thump.

A precordial thump involves the resuscitator taking his or her fist and using it like a sledge hammer hitting the patient's sternum (breast bone). The theory behind a precordial thump was to give the heart a "jump start." I never understood this theory but the protocol had been beaten into my head over the past ten to twenty years. Whenever I hit any other muscle in the body all that ever resulted was pain and later a bruise. I never once punched my legs then magically started running. Evidence supporting the use of sternal thumps was, at best, sketchy. But, I figured what the heck, I've got nothing to lose. If a precordial thump could revive Ethan Hunt in Mission Impossible III surely it'd work on this dude (that would be total sarcasm, in case you were wondering).

The overhead cabin lights were on, everybody was either sitting up in their seats or leaning into the aisle to see what was going on. I guess that despite the passenger induced turbulence, the fasten seatbelt sign was either turned off or being completely ignored. So I jumped up almost touching the ceiling, clinched my fist and brought the hammer down crashing it into his chest. I hit him so hard his feet flew two or three feet off the ground. He sat up, grabbed his chest and yelled "What the hell is going on here?" The on looking passengers all erupted in spontaneous cheering. I felt like a Superbowl MVP Quarterback as I walked back to my seat. Passengers were giving me high fives while others said, "Nice job Angela's dad. Good job…"

As I sat down I noticed a woman reading a Dermatology journal. She looked at me and said, "I would not have been any help back there unless you needed advice on a skin cancer on the top of his head." A few minutes later the stewardess informed me that the Captain wanted to speak with me. Angela got handed off again. I thought that the Captain was going to give me a metal or a coupon for a free flight. Instead he asked me how serious was the revived passenger's condition? I informed the Captain that he was not breathing, his lips were purple and he had no pulses. My best guess was that he had a cardiac arrest from either an arrhythmia or a pulmonary embolus from a deep vein thrombosis (common issues that were exacerbated by air travel). The Captain thanked me then said, "You might want to get back to your seat now. I'll give you a few minutes". Well, that wasn't what I was expecting. A few minutes later, the Captain announced that we had to make an emergency landing in Albuquerque, New Mexico (the closest airport) so that the passenger in the back could receive appropriate medical care, not that mine was totally inappropriate. Suddenly, my status as a cult hero was magically transformed into an international terrorist. This stop meant that over half of the passengers would miss their connecting flights. Several passengers might not even make it home on Christmas Day. Angela's dad was now in deep dog doo-doo. Had parachutes been available, Mr. Fat Guy and I would have been promptly ejected.

Mr. Dead as a Doornail Fat Guy protested vehemently that nothing was wrong as he was escorted from the plane via stretcher to the ambulance waiting nearby. In retrospect maybe he was just sleeping. When I finally got home my brother reminded me that he used to snore like a B52 bomber with all four engines revving up. His girlfriend after college forced him to get a sleep apnea study because she couldn't sleep at night. She said the snoring didn't bother her. What kept her awake was the anxiety of his prolonged breath holding. She would often shake him to wake him up and force a deep breath. His sleep study results were mind boggling. He held his breath 108 times during the night with the average apneic period lasting one minute and ten seconds. The longest breath holding stretch lasted 8 minutes and 32 seconds. I'm like, "Dude, I knew you had brain damage but that's ridiculous." He has used a Continuous Positive Airway Pressure (CPAP) machine for sleep ever since. Maybe Mr. Christmas Eve pot belly dead as a doornail passenger just had sleep apnea. Hopefully not, that would ruin the story. By the way, the

American Heart Association has recently removed pre-cordial thumps as a recommended intervention.

While on holiday I decided to visit my beloved undergraduate college. I was walking around campus when I noticed that the same Psychology Professor who gave me the Rorschach Test was now the Dean of Academics. I stepped into the Administrative office and mentioned to the secretary that if Dr. Pierce wasn't too busy tell her that Pancho Hammer would love to say hello. Word came back immediately and I was escorted inside. She explained that she could remember some students with amazing clarity and I was one. She named the High School I went to, the Graduate Program I was accepted to and a few other minor details. I informed her that I took her sage advice about Medical School. I went back and did three years of undergraduate coursework, five years of Medical School, six years of Residency, one year of Fellowship training and now I sit in my office all day listening to patients complain about problems they don't really want to get fixed. The difference was that the pay was a lot better being a spine surgeon as compared to a clinical psychologist.

Without disclosing confidential patient information, I told Dr. Pierce of a 56 year old obese female who I evaluated for chronic back pain. She was barely five feet tall and buried the needle on our 320 pound maximum scale. She was actually larger than Mr. Christmas Eve airline passenger. I was trying not to be too judgmental. She could have had cancer of the spine, a herniated disk or some other legitimate problem that may have required surgical intervention. I entered the room, introduced myself, shook her hand and asked: "What is your main complaint?" She looked at me without blinking an eye and said, "My back hurts so much I can only make one trip through the buffet." Without blinking an eye, Mr. Compassionate responded, "Ma'am, I would call that… a clue."

Needing a break from such patients I took a position as the camp physician at the South Pole. The Base at the South Pole was staffed by 75-80 people who served one year rotations. Tony Baloney would be working there as an astrophysicist studying the effects of gamma rays on the ozone. I had only seen him once or twice in the past five or six years so this was a great opportunity to reconnect. The isolation also gave me time to finish writing a few research articles and work on some inventions. Dick Steele went to the Morgue, I went to the South Pole.

Adjusting to life at the South Pole takes time. The sun was visible all day long for six months, then invisible for the following six months. One cold long summer day, one really cold long winter night, and a few weeks of transition. Rotations at the South Pole started during the early part of summer for several reasons. The first reason involved safety. Landing planes during daylight was challenging. Attempting to land an airplane in total darkness with no true runway was suicide. Retrieving dropped supplies during the darkness was dangerous enough. Night drops only occurred for emergencies. Those driving

the snowmobiles to retrieve the packages described
the rides as both exhilarating and terrifying. I was
also amazed (and terrified) at how hard it was to light
a barrel of (cold) gasoline on fire for these drops. The
second reason yearly shifts started in early summer
was that the lighted days allowed for the
identification of individuals who did not adjust.
Solitude, like retirement, always sounds great but
confinement makes some individuals anxious.
Agitation coupled with sleep deprivation and
confinement can ignite insanity. For safety reasons,
individuals who decompensated had to be evacuated
early. Six months of ambient darkness, on the other
hand, can magnify the inner darkness making
depression and drinking problems significantly
worse. Drinkers and depressives were harder to
identify early so you had to live with them, and count
the days until sunlight.

I always used exercise to fend off depression and
this strategy continued working at the South Pole.
During the summer Tony and I would take turns
racing the only bicycle around the compound. The
winner would get the other guy's desert that night.
Onlookers would think that that desert was the best
chocolate cake or scoop of ice cream ever eaten. Each
savored bite would be followed by deep moans of
delight. It was ceremonial gloating at its best (and
worst). Another important, but usually boring,
ceremony that everyone participated in at the South
Pole was on January first. The base commander gave
a speech, pulled the Pole out of the ice, identified the

current geographic South Pole then replanted the pole. During its rotation around the Sun the Earth wobbled, so every year the geographic location of the South Pole shifted.

The transition from 24 hours of daylight to continuous darkness had just begun. Coinciding with the loss of sunlight was a significant drop in temperature. Most nights the temperature was well below zero. As the temperature got closer to $-100°F$ South Pole veterans came calling: "Are you in or out?" On a few precious nights, when the winds were calm, first timers to the South Pole could be initiated into Club 300, the dumbest club ever.

The fraternity was called Club 300 because that's the difference between the outside temperature ($-100°F$) and the temperature inside the sauna ($+200°F$). Two or three pledges sat naked in the sauna drinking water for 10-15 minutes in order to work up a good sweat and stretch their muscles. Just before exiting the sauna they would dry their feet and put on socks and shoes. They'd bust out of the sauna and grab a flashlight. Fanatics lined the pathway from the sauna to the exiting door. Two people held the door open and everyone cheered and yelled for good luck. Pledges rushed out into the frigid darkness to run one lap around the South Pole. The temperature dropped quickly at night so only one or two groups could safely join the Fraternity on any given night. No attempts were made if it was windy outside.

Three groups of pledges had made successful entries into Club 300. Two pledges took one step outside and ran back into the sauna. The window of opportunity was slipping away when Tony came into my office. "I'll do it if you do it," he said. Incredulously I said, "Tony, Club 300 is the dumbest F'ing thing I've ever heard of. What time?" It was 2 pm and we were sitting in the sauna. It was pitch black outside and the temperature was falling. Our D-Day (D for Defrost) was scheduled to start in about 10 minutes. I don't know if I was sweating because it was so hot in the sauna or because I was so nervous. I told Tony that if I was leading when we got there that I was not stopping for a quick pole dance. I saw what happened to Flick in a Christmas Story and I would not chance having Mr. Happiness stuck to the South Pole. Imagine that call to the company commander explaining how the pole got dislodged. Worse yet, the phone call home explaining how the good doctor died frozen to the South Pole doing a cheesy night club act. I laced up my shoes and took a couple deep breaths. A hand waved at us from outside the sauna window. Five, four, three, two, one and we're off. I heard the cheers, saw the door open, grabbed a flashlight and sprinted outside into the darkness. One might think that being mostly naked in -100oF temperatures would be really cold. Ironically, as soon as we stepped outside the sweat from being in the sauna froze and we were instantly insulated. Praise Allah.

We heard the door slam behind us and when we turned around to look we lost directional focus. Now I could see the South Pole from my office window. I looked at it every single day. It was probably 50 yards from my office and 25 from the door we just exited. But it was pitch black. The pole wasn't illuminated and the flashlights were for us to shine on the ground so we wouldn't trip over a block of ice or twist an ankle in a crevice. We both realized that we had been out way too long (maybe 10 seconds). We had probably ran 50-60 yards already. The trip back would put us well over 100 yards total. We decided that the smartest thing to do was run to the closest door to get inside. The problem was that one of us would have to grab the frozen door knob to twist it open. I got there first and grabbed the knob and opened the door. Tony's lungs had started to freeze so he was a few yards behind. The hand frozen to the flashlight was no big deal. The hand frozen to the door knob was worrisome. No time to think, I just ripped my hand off the knob. If you've ever accidently put your hand on a hot stove you know the immediate and brain consuming pain of degloving all the skin off the palmar surface of your hand.

I told Dr. Pierce that the cost for that adventure was the skin off my left hand and some reversible frostbite on the manfinger. Not enough game day shrinkage I guess. Tony got a pneumonia and reversible frostbite on several fingertips. Two weeks of recovery and all was back to normal. Nothing had to be amputated, Praise Allah. This adventure proved to me the power of peer pressure over sound medical advice. Years later Tony would serve as camp commander of the South Pole. Thereafter we introduced him as Toney Baloney, former Mayor of South Park, sounds even better.

Dr. Pierce was also a cat lover so I told her a story from my personal life. I was at a Hospital Christmas party when I saw three single women walk across the dance floor. One had on a black mini skirt, purple shear blouse, black ankle high boots with three inch heels and auburn red hair. Before I could track her down she disappeared. The following week I asked one of the techs if she knew this mystery woman? She did and agreed to extend an invitation for a date on my behalf. The messenger returned a few days later with some unfortunate news. The Sweet Thang was in a relationship. I thanked the messenger and we went about our business.

A few months later the Sweet Thang was working on our side of the hospital. The operating rooms for Orthopedic and heart surgeries were geographically separated. I walked into the OR where she was setting up for a case. "Hello" I said, "I'm the guy who asked about you. If things don't work out with your boyfriend I'd love to go out with you." That was the first and only time I have seen her embarrassed. I ran into her in the hallway a few months later and she was wearing an LSU Football sweatshirt. We joyfully reminisced about our time on the Bayou. Word came from the messenger a few months later that she was available. Our first date was on September 11, 2001. Yes, that September 11th (9/11). I like to tell my friends that, at least for me, she compensated for all the unhappiness on that day.

The Sweet Thang had two cats, Clyde and Striker. Striker was terrified of everyone and hid under the bed the first year we dated. He eventually came to like me and would hang out. Clyde, on the other hand, was a troll from day 1. He would hiss at me until the day he died, even when I was feeding him. By the second or third time I spent the night at Sweet Thang's place I determined that I enjoyed the upstairs shower more than the downstairs one. It was an old fashioned shower inside a tub but the water pressure was better than the fancier water conservation showerhead downstairs.

I got out of bed and headed upstairs to take a shower. Sweet Thang had already left for work. Clyde had left me a present in the upstairs shower. A clear and concise fecal message that I was not welcomed. After cleaning it up I thought, well his cat box was right there across from the shower. I'll leave him a message he won't ever forget. Fortunately, I reconsidered as the Sweet Thang and I were still very early in our relationship. Cleaning up that cat box message may have been a deal breaker. You see, every now and then I did exercise good judgment.

We eventually got married. Dr. Pierce could not believe that we dated 15 years before tying the knot. I confessed that I was terrified of marriage. Almost everyone I knew said that things changed after getting married. And things really changed after having children. I told Dr. Pierce of the two and only two romantic things Sweet Thang ever did say about us. The first comment was to one of her friends who was adamant that we marry after a year of dating. She told her friend that because we were not married we made the choice to be together every day. The second item of romance came years later when I asked her why she never pushed the getting married issue. She said that she made the decision early in our relationship that she was going to be with me whether we were married or not. I'm anxiously awaiting the third.

When I introduce her to people now I rarely say, "This is my wife..." but rather, "meet my ex-girlfriend..." When the Sweet Thang and I (finally) got married, we had all of our accidental friends (or their husbands) representing the Flying Elvises. And, what Las Vegas Elvis themed wedding would be complete without karaoke at the reception? Most people would rather listen to their neighbors mowing their lawns than me singing. I'm sure that all living and dead members of Lynyrd Skynyrd were cosmically cringing as I butchered Sweet Home Alabama by singing "Sweet Thang Louisiana, Lord I'm coming home to you..."

The third interesting Sweet Thang related story occurred after the South Pole adventure. I returned back to my Academic post but one of my hospital privilege forms wasn't filed appropriately. I had only worked at this particular hospital for six years. My badge still opened all secured doors. Didn't matter, I had to reapply as if I had never worked there before. Granted, I did not work there often. I only provided coverage for a fellow Spine surgeon when he needed a vacation or had an out of town conference to attend. Nine months later and three cancelled interviews I informed my friend that I was not going to cancel another day of clinic or surgery just to have the AdminisTraitor cancel on me at the last minute. As my fellow spine surgeon had a vacation scheduled the following week I magically got an appointment that afternoon.

There were two items delaying the reappointment. The first was that I refused to allow them to perform a financial credit check. I was not applying for employment, an auto loan, or a home equity loan. And it was none of their business as far as I was concerned. The AdminisTraitor agreed. The credit check was placed in the application as more and more physicians were becoming hospital employees. The second item of contention was even more ridiculous. Sweet Thang and I were now "living in sin". As a result computer generated junk mail came to our house addressed to someone with my first name and her last name (Dr. Pancho Thang). The Hospital AdminisTraitor accused me of having an alias — a separate identity. The following week I started an advertising campaign on small (236 ml) milk cartons in the Doctor's Lounge. Many thought it was hysterically funny, some I'm sure wished it were true.

Moral of the stories: always choose your dumping grounds, pole dances, and advertising venues carefully.

Chapter 13

Clydesdales and Cardboard Signs

Sweet Thang was an anesthesia provider who could handle impatient men with large egos. She had worked with the heart surgeons who did the first human heart transplants, the heart surgeons who performed the first artificial heart transplants, and she put up with me. This talent meant that she usually worked with the most difficult surgeon in the OR on any given day. One day she was working with a Pain Management doctor and asked him what he was doing that weekend. He said that he was doing a Triathlon in Florida. She said she'd look for him as her boyfriend (i.e., me) was doing the same race. Big Al, the Clydesdale Champion became Accidental Friend number ten.

The water was warm, probably low 80's F. How the swim was declared wet suit legal was beyond comprehension. Wet suits improved swimmer floatation, making it much harder to drown. Wet suits might also taste bad to alligators. There had been two alligator attacks in the lake we were swimming in the week before the race. I usually swam outside the pack to avoid getting (accidentally) kicked or punched. Not for that race. I tried to position myself in the middle of the pack. The theory was that the swimmers on the outsides would get dragged under first. Good idea but every time another swimmer's hand touched my foot I thought I was a goner. This was the only event in which I was sweating profusely when I got out of the drink.

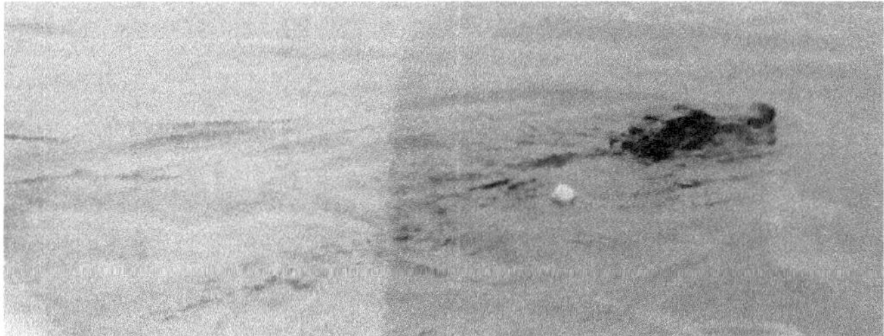

The ambient temperature was over 110°F for most of the day. I got off the bike ready to run but only made it a few steps before my ears felt like someone lit them on fire. I had to walk the entire first mile and most of all miles until mile 22. The sun finally set when I reached mile 22, the temperature dropped into the 90's and I was able to jog the final 4 miles.

Big Al decided we should race in Europe as well. He and Emma decided to go to Wimbledon to see some tennis before heading to IM Austria. Sweet Thang and I started in Austria with travel plans after the race. Big Al told us that they had missed half a day of Wimbledon as their train was delayed. A businessman had committed suicide earlier that morning. In England it was tradition for businessmen committing suicide to remove his shoes, place them on the side of the railroad tracks then sit down and wait. The high speed train would handle it from there. Wrestlers often took their shoes off and left them on the mat after finishing their last match. The gesture signified they were retired. Maybe the British Businessman suicide tradition was started by a former wrestler.

It was unseasonably hot in Klagenfurt. This made sleeping difficult. The air conditioning inside Austrian hotels consisted of opening up the windows and hoping for a breeze. To make matters worse, World Cup soccer matches were being broadcasted in the plaza. Bull horns and intermittent cheering or booing kept us up all night. I had reserved a bicycle for the race as shipping mine internationally was cost prohibitive. I usually rode a size 56, the rental bike was a size 52 but I didn't have any other options. My knees were millimeters away from hitting the handle bars with every revolution. Realizing that I was not going to have a good bike split I rationalized that I would just have to make up time on the run.

Big Al jumped in the lake as soon as the starting cannon sounded. Al enjoyed the contact and would have been a professional wrestler if his father would have approved. I waited for the chaos of the mass start to calm down. I got out of the water before him but he saw me in the transition tent, AKA the sausage factory. Wellington, also doing the race, passed me at mile 25 and said he was feeling good. I was making pretty good progress on my Toys-R-Us bicycle and caught him at mile 80. Wellington had a bad habit of forgetting to drink on the bike. Consequently, he dehydrated really early in the race.

Most days Wellington could catch me on the run. I figured that I might have a 5-10 minute lead by the time he rehydrated and started the three-loop run course. The transition area and the finish line were right by the lake. The run course started near the beach and sand volleyball courts. One delightful mile later, the course turned right and we passed through some rental apartment complexes then paralleled the train tracks. Three miles later racers ran through the plaza then a shaded run creek side back to the transition area and finish line. I calculated that Wellington would catch me within the first ten miles of the marathon. I told myself that I would run a good pace until he caught me then I'd jog it in to the finish. Mile ten passed without a Wellington sighting.

Mile fifteen passed, again no Wellington. Amazingly, I saw him and Big Al ahead of me at mile 20, walking.

They were on run lap #2 and I was on lap #3. Wellington said that the bonk on the bicycle was worse than expected. He had been walking since mile 9. Big Al was plugging along at his own pace and was enjoying Wellington's company. They planned on alternating walking and jogging the rest of the marathon. That is, unless one of them decided to take their shoes off, sit on the train tracks and wait for the six o'clock. The only other time Wellington forgot to rehydrate he had calf cramps so bad he to walk the entire marathon. He finished at 11:59 pm (one minute before the midnight cut off). We spent the entire night in the Emergency Room getting him rehydrated. His serum potassium was 6.6 mmol. He was lucky he didn't have a cardiac arrhythmia and die.

After IM Austria we went to Vienna so that I could see Freud's house and museum (one of my bucket list items). After visiting with Sigmund, we were off to France to see the Tour. Sweet Thang got to see her beloved Lancy-poo in Le Tour. She had a shirt which read "The happiest day of my life" in honor of the New Orleans Saints winning Superbowl XLIV (44). I should have gotten her a shirt in France that read "The second happiest day of my life" with a picture of the Tour in the background. We stood for over 5 hours in 104°F heat fighting odiferous French elders for 10 seconds of a bicycling blur. At least she checked something off her bucket list.

Speaking of buckets, hyperkalemia and the
Saints… Sweet Thang's dad, the Buffalo, was up in
years and fairly poor health. He was not allowed to
watch Saints games live for fear of having another
heart attack. Sweet Thang traditionally called him
every Sunday. She called him that Sunday from
Paris. He said, "Heard y'all were in Paris. I was there
at the end of the war (World War II)". Later that
month he drove himself to the Veterans Affairs
Hospital with indigestion. He was admitted, labs
were drawn, by the time his potassium returned at 6.9
he experienced a cardiac arrhythmia and died.
Wellington's physiology could tolerate the high
potassium, the Buffalo's could not.

The following year Big Al, the Clydesdale
Champion, talked us into running the Bourbon Chase.
The Bourbon Chase was a 48 hour 235 mile relay
through the Kentucky backwoods. Each team had six
runners who alternated splits. Running on narrow
country roads in the middle of the night was
frightening and yes, stupid. Maybe not Club 300
stupid but close. No one worried about frostbite, just

getting mowed over by a car or truck going 70 mph. Runners and teams would be disqualified for wearing headphones. Even without headphones, all that I could hear was the dueling banjos from Deliverance.

The Tri Knox was another stupid triathlon Big Al talked us into doing. The race wasn't stupid per say, but we were for doing it. The race day forecast was for thunder storms. Many of the country roads had flooded the day before. The race directors moved transition from its usual area to a parking garage so that our equipment could be as dry as possible. Maximillian flew in for the race and we all went out carbo loading the night before. We all thought that the race would cancelled for safety reasons. So we ate spicy food for dinner and ice cream for desert. To our utter amazement the race proceeded. The Tennessee River water was 68°F and Maximillian nearly drowned. Someone clocked him with a left hook to the jaw and he swallowed a large amount of water. His goggles were nowhere to be found and he had to swim the last half mile without them. Visibility on the bike was awful, it was raining so hard. Who knows if the brakes would have worked if needed. Having lived in Louisiana I have been guilty of driving an automobile through deep water, but I'd never been stupid enough to ride a bicycle through deep water until that day.

Fortunately, the rain stopped and by the end of the bike ride the sun popped out. I left the parking garage with dry shoes, dry socks and pruned feet. The course took us out by the football stadium on the way to the greenway (paved sidewalk next to a creek). I ran zig-zags to dodge the puddles while the guys coming back towards the finish line were running straight hitting every puddle in line. They weren't making any effort to avoid them. By the time I got to the greenway I understood. The creek had overflowed. We had to run in eight to ten inches of water for one mile on the way out and one mile on the way back. I didn't bother dodging the puddles when I got back near the stadium either. I was just glad that my feet thawed out during the run.

The following year we signed up for a race in Germany. Sweet Thang took us on a historical death march the week before the race. Brandenburg Plaza, Check Point Charlie, the Reichstag, the Topography of Terror museum, a walking tour of the Third Reich, the Berlin Wall, and of course, what uplifting parade of happiness would be complete without a visit to a concentration camp. Now, I don't normally go to Gestapo Headquarters or concentration camps the day before Ironman races, but when I'm in Berlin, I prefer Sachenhausen. The inscription "Arbeit Mach Frei" — "Work shall make you free" was inscribed at the entrance to all concentration camps. I've often thought of having that inscription placed at the entrance to my basement gym and bedroom. I call the place the Pain Cave. Sweet Thang calls it the same thing but for other reasons I'm sure.

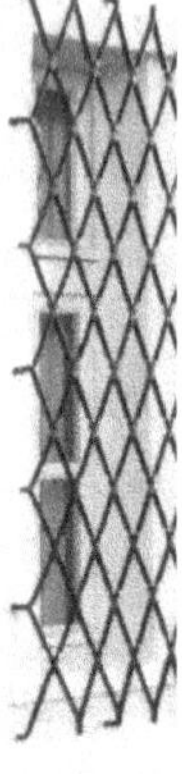

We joked about the river swim because anyone seen
swimming in the river during the war was shot at, no
questions asked. It's amazing how a little historical
knowledge or context can change the perspective of a
race.

Cold water swims outside of Florida seemed to be
a trend and IM Coeur d'Alene was no exception. Big
Al chose this race so that he could take the family up
into Montana and Wyoming afterwards. The lake
had freezing cold water, two to three foot swells, and
strong cross winds. In preparation for the prolonged
ice bath I bought a thick neoprene hoodie and scuba
gloves. Unfortunately, scuba gloves were not allowed
in IM races and the hoodie caused water to leak into
my goggles. My left eye was blurred for most of the
112 miles on the bike. I ran well, even though some
chicken broth at mile 18 of the run gave me severe
abdominal cramping and the fear of explosive race
course diarrhea. Being a veteran I used a port-a-let to
relieve the gastric unpleasantries. When this hot chic
racer was stretching her calf muscles on the side of

the road a spectator commented: "looking good." She smiled back and said, "Thanks, but I just shit myself." I felt her pain (but not her shame).

Once again I came upon a fellow athlete with similar outrageous fashion. We passed one another for at least 8 miles on the run. We then had a come to Jesus meeting around mile 23. He was 20 years my junior. I was now the overweight Mexican in the photo but with only two nipples instead of three. When asked how his race was going he confided that he too got very cold during the swim. He had stayed in the warming tent for 36 minutes. Warming tent? Had I known about a warming tent I may have stayed in there for an hour. I told him there was no glory sprinting past an old fat guy down the shoot, so we had a blast finishing together.

Big Al, Maximillian and I did IM Lake Placid the following July. Instead of concentration camps, we visited the Winter Olympics Museum and rode the Bobsled course. Sweet Thang didn't want to wake up at 5 AM to give me a ride to transition so I went to the front desk and asked to borrow a magic maker and cardboard box. I then wrote: "Homeless racer. Need ride to start line. God bless." Sweet Thang was mortified, but at least she agreed to give me a ride to the race start the following morning. The course was amazingly beautiful and extremely challenging. My knees hurt for a year after that race.

Sweet Thang and I had a history of cardboard signs. One year she ran for State Representative. She had signs and shirts made for advertising. I actually wore a shirt for the marathon portion of our local triathlon (got big brownie points for that surprise). During another brownie point collection event, I secretly arranged with her best friend to pick her up at the airport. She had been to a national conference and was flying back to another part of the state where her state association was meeting. I greeted her with an election poster with duct tape covering the "Elect" and "for State Representative" parts and wrote in "Marry Me?"

She liked that sign and surprise much more than the time the sign read: "Welcome Home from Rehab."

Moral of the stories: Time and context determine our perspective of reality.

Chapter 14
Yaking and Getting Lei'd

Maximillian has had his share of injuries as well. Five weeks before IM 70.3 St. George he twisted his ankle while running. He sent me a photograph asking for treatment recommendations. I recommend that he go to the hospital as the ankle was so swollen I thought it was fractured. X-rays were negative and he was diagnosed with a grade 4 ligament sprain. He was given crutches and instructed to be non-weight bearing with crutches for six weeks.

Two weeks before the race his ankle was still so swollen that he could not fit it into a shoe. Any pressure on the sole of the foot or toes caused immense pain. I recommend that he either abandon the race or do a relay. St. George was one of a few places were two or three person teams could divide and conquer the course. The relay slots were full and they would not refund his entry fee. It was also too late to cancel the plane ticket. I advised him to leave his running shoes at home. I knew how competitive he was and if he saw everyone else running he would lace up his shoes and give it a go. The only bad thing about just doing the swim and the bike was that you would be listed as a DNF (did not finish). No results for any part of the race completed would be published in the final standings, just a DNF. One week before the race and he started weight bearing and his foot could fit his foot inside a shoe.

I picked up my rental bike. The size was correct but it was a hybrid road/mountain bike with 27 gears, not a racing bike with aerobars built for speed. No worries I thought, St. George was a hilly course and the smaller gears should have worked to my advantage. We call this ego defense mechanism, rationalization. Besides, Maximillian would either not do the run or walk it, so the Hammer was not in jeopardy, or so I thought. The morning of the race all was going well. We got to the body marking area just outside of transition where my race number was inscribed on my arms. When asked my age I jokingly replied: "97". Much to our amazement the volunteer actually wrote 97 on my left calf.

While lining up for the swim start and I felt uneasy. For whatever reason my brain was telling me NOT put my face into the water. Naturally, I jumped right in. Then it hit me as to why my unconscious mind didn't want me to submerge my face. The water was freezing cold. Ironman St. George was always wet suit legal so the coldness was no surprise. It was when the freezing cold water got into my ear canal that the realization of the warning materialized. The world started spinning out of control. The technical term for this is vertigo. I thought for sure I was going to drown. Fortunately, I dog paddled over to a kayak and held on. After a few minutes I tried swimming again. The vertigo got worse. This time the vertigo was accompanied with projectile vomiting. A race Marshall came over in a power boat as he heard the retching 50 yards away. Swimmers stopped to look around because the retching was so loud. The Marshall encouraged me to get into the

boat. Knowing that getting into the boat would
disqualify me from the race, I said, "It's not this
clown's first rodeo. Just give me a few minutes. I'm
swimming from kayak to kayak (truly in between the
yaks). If I get into trouble I'll raise my arm and clinch
my fist." He believed me and let me finish. The truth
was that I didn't want a DNF next to my name and I
didn't want to relinquish the Hammer to Maximillian
or Tony.

As I got out of the water I staggered to my bike like
a drunk at closing time. I plopped down beside the
bike and waited for the nausea to get better.
Swimming with vertigo was pretty stupid. There was
definitely a chance I could have drowned. But riding
a bike with vertigo would guarantee a trip to the local
Emergency Room accompanied with weeks of
excruciating pain from the road rash and whatever
else might break. I managed to drink a bottle of
Gatorade and headed out slowly on the bike. Having
a 97 written on my leg afforded me great respect
during the race especially in those first few miles
when my speed, approximately 10 mph, was
consistent with other 97 year-old racers. By mile 30 I
had recovered and resumed my normal 20 mph pace
on the flats. Many racers provided cheerful words of
encouragement. One guy pulled up next to me and
said, "Man, you're 50 years older than me, riding a
mountain bike and you're still kicking my ass." I told
him that the Red Bull gave me wings. Red Bull and
Gatorade were the official drinks of Ironman at the
time.

The only good thing about being sick early in the race was that if you recovered you could finish strong. I had exerted very little energy swimming and biking, compared to other races, so I had plenty of energy left for the run. In fact, I ran rather well. St. George was a two lap run with lots of elevation. I had seen Big Al and Tony Baloney on the run but not Maximillian. I figured he wisely stopped after the bike. Nope, he was out there running, I just hadn't seen him. I crossed the finish line and asked Sweet Thang as to Maximillian's location. She said that according to the tracker he would be finishing in about 20 minutes. Sure enough, 20 minutes later Maximillian came trotting across the finish line. He was now the one concluding how much stronger peer pressure was compared to sound medical advice. Ironically his ankle was less swollen at the end of the race than at the beginning.

As competitive as Maximillian and I were, we did not hold a candle to Wellington. One year Wellington won the Hammer at the Vineman 70.3. He then took the ceremonial post race photo of us bowing to the Hammer and bought a full page ad in the New England Observer with the caption, "Congratulations Maximillian, All Hail the Hammer."

Maximillian was unaware of the newspaper clip until one of his neighbors brought it to his attention. He said he was confused because the guy claiming victory with his arms above his head didn't look like him. Maximillian explained that he was one of the guys bowing and that Wellington was the one claiming victory. They decided the best revenge was to never mention (to Wellington) that they had ever seen the ad. For two years Maximillian said nothing to Wellington. It was right after the IM Galveston 70.3 race when Maximillian's daughter said, "Hey Dad isn't that the guy from the newspaper?" Although delayed, Wellington claimed victory again.

Wellington's third and most epic victory came on his wedding night. The celebration was marked with elegance and extravagance. No expense was spared bringing in Champagne and various wines from around the world to the event. As the best man, Maximillian gave a heart-warming toast recounting several funny stories that bonded the two together. As Maximillian spoke, Wellington was plotting. Revenge is never a straight line and Wellington had paid a server to make sure that Maximillian's glass was never half empty. Who would have thought that after the reception the limo driver would take Wellington and Maximillian to Quadburn Hill. And, who other than Wellington, would have had a pair of running shoes planted in the limo for just such an event. By the time Maximillian realized they were at Quadburn Hill Wellington had sprinted half way to the top. Maximillian was drunk, still donning a full tuxedo and dress shoes, when he stumbled uphill to bitter defeat.

As fate would have it, Tony, Big Al and I all qualified for IM Hawaii in 2016. Without doubt, it was the greatest bucket list experiences of my life. I tell people that doing the race was surreal. I had watched The Ironman World Championships on television for 30 years and now I was there. The experience would be similar for a golfer who got paired with Tiger Woods or Jack Nicolaus during the Masters. Or, a speed demon getting to drive during the Indy 500.

When Tony Baloney, the Mayor of South Park, requalified in 2018 we were celebrating the next day at our favorite Monday night hangout. I stood up and raised my glass for a toast. "Your attention please" I said while tapping the side of the glass. "I would like to congratulate everyone who finished yesterday but more importantly, at approximately

11:30 this morning Tony got lei'd for the first time in two years. And, as a result, his beautiful wife is getting another trip to Hawaii as compensation." You see, when one qualifies for Hawaii they put a lei around your neck during the awards ceremony. Any day you can finish an Ironman is a great day. Any day you get lei'd as a result of finishing an Ironman is a really great day. So get you minds out of the gutter and start training.

Given that Maximillian and I had nearly drowned during IM races, Wellington thought it appropriate that we go white water rafting down the Colorado River for his 50th birthday. Wellington and his ten best friends all met in Las Vegas. We rented a van and drove to Utah. We went to the sporting goods store and picked up life preservers and helmets (again). Stories of Glenwood Creeeeeeeeek started resurfacing. Wellington said that the American River was nothing compared to the Colorado River. Maximillian was not too worried because the rafts were motorized. Only kayaks and paddle rafts flipped over, or so we thought. The guide informed us that if the boat flipped to stay calm and try to swim to the side.

The first day was fairly mild, a few class 3 rapids and some hiking. We enjoyed hamburgers and hot dogs by campfire along with a birthday cake for Wellington. The night was peaceful and as there were no street lights we gazed at the million stars above until we drifted off to sleep. The next morning we packed up, ate breakfast, and headed down river.

The class 4 rapids did not disappoint. It was easy to see why the early settlers would pull their boats out of the water and carry them around the rapids. Although we were never in any danger of capsizing, the boat definitely slammed into the water after going over the larger waves. One could easily imagine how the wooden boats of old with deep hulls would have been destroyed instantly.

Wellington asked the guide if we could hop out of the boat and go down the rapids by ourselves. The guide agreed so long as we waited until a class 3 rapid before we "fell" overboard. As soon as we got the word Wellington slid overboard. Maximillian not wanting to be outdone slid off the other side. I jumped as far off the side of the boat as I could so as not to get hit by the boat or motor. Obtaining a lot of momentum before hitting the water was a bad idea. I hit the water and even with a life vest tightly secured the current pushed me downstream a good 50 yards before I could surface and get my first gasp of air. Should you readers ever find yourselves outside the boat heading for the rapids, remember this one life saving piece of advice: always take your breath (breathe in) while in the wave's trough. Intuitively you'll want to try to inhale at the wave's peak. The problem is (gravity) you rarely make it to the peak before the wave submerges you. Attempting to breathe at the peak results in a pair of lungs full of water. If you were to survive and be rescued the ensuing pneumonia would probably kill you. For legal purposes I have to recommend that you never willingly leave your boat or do any of the other really stupid life threatening things described in this book (unless, of course, you too have brain damaged accidental friends like I do who find pleasure in trying to kill you, so you have too).

Moral of the stories: racing and adventures are fun, especially if you get lei'd afterwards.

Chapter 15
Men Packing Heat and Ice Cream

As fate would have it, I finally became Chairman of the Department. The Chief had retired and the replacement Chairman did not fare so well. We left the great Mid-West and headed back down to Gulf Coast University. No one from Gulf Coast University Orthopedics had published a scientific article in almost a decade. The department hired Claudia, a PhD from Royale, to work with the Residents. Just before I was scheduled to start as Chairman four abstracts were accepted to the Academy's annual meeting. Our research Resident the previous year was a talented female from Columbia with a strong engineering background. Her name was Guadalupe, Lupe for short.

It was my first official day as Chairman. I was unpacking my stuff from cardboard boxes when I noticed two men sitting in the back of the room. Both were wearing dark suits with white shirts and black ties. I was sure they were both packing heat. "May I help you?" I inquired. One of them answered in the affirmative. As I was now the official Department Chairman they wanted to interview me first to determine which leads to follow. Claudia, the director of research, had come to work the previous Friday morning but left early. The lab was often empty by noon on Fridays. I surmised that everyone had finished their experiments or had tests running on autopilot. Many orthopedic devices underwent 5-

10 million cycles during destructive testing. Some devices can take two weeks to complete a biomechanical test. Tests were often set up so they could run over the weekend. Turns out Claudia had lots of unscheduled tests that weekend (CT scans, CBC, chemistry 20, etc...). She made a detour through the Emergency Room as she wasn't feeling well enough to drive home. Magnum PI and his sidekick Perry Mason explained that Claudia was on life support in the ICU.

I agreed to gather information that night from the staff physicians at the Chairman's Welcoming Dinner. I would then interview the Residents Tuesday before Fracture Conference. At the Chairman's dinner I found out that Claudia had been double dipping. Claudia and her long term girlfriend were living together. When Lupe went into the lab the two of them were exchanging more than just scientific ideas. The Residents confirmed the affair allegations. When I asked Lupe if she knew anything about Claudia her response was: "do I need to hire a lawyer?"

I called Katrina for advice on what to do next. She knew Claudia from Royale and had plenty of experience running a department. I was recounting the story when she stopped me and said, "Pancho, she poisoned her. It's very common in Columbia. Lupe probably put Ethylene Glycol (antifreeze) in Claudia's coffee or Gatorade." Sure enough, traces of Ethylene Glycol were found in Claudia's coffee cup. She went to the ER feeling nauseous and her serum creatinine was going through the roof (indicative of kidney failure). Lupe got 10 years for attempted murder. She would have gotten life had Claudia gone home and died. As Freddie Mercury and Queen once said: "Another one (Orthopedic Resident) bites the dust."

One of the best things about being Chairman at a prestigious university, was the travel. There was no shortage of invitations to speak at graduations, conferences or policy meetings. The Chief loved trips to Santa Fe, New Mexico but the Sweet Thang loved international travel. We were honored guests at the Orthopedic Spine Annual Conference, Pacific Division in Japan. Sweet Thang's sister flew into to take care of the kids as we planned an extended vacation afterwards. I went down to the lobby to grab a couple Starbucks but my credit card was denied. I handed the cashier some Yen then headed back to the room. The conference started in five minutes so I asked Sweet Thang to look into the credit card issue.

At the morning break Sweet Thang informed me that the credit card company denied the coffee because they thought the card had been stolen. Just before the Starbucks charge in Japan, $512 had been charged to the card from our home computer. Angela, now six, received a computer game called "Belle of the Ball" for Christmas. It appeared that she had purchased several dresses, pairs of shoes and tickets to attend a virtual gala at Buckingham Palace. I was reluctant for her to accept the gift and this confirmed my suspicion of corporations preying on minors. Sweet Thang and I had agreed that one of us was to supervise her at all times while she was playing so this wouldn't happen. Angela must have been playing unsupervised. I was really pissed off and demanded that Sweet Thang rectify the situation before I got back from the afternoon session.

I was listening to a talk on growth factors used during lumbar fusions when I got a text message from Sweet Thang. Angela's game was linked through my E-mail account and she needed the password. I texted back the password still seething in anger. By the time I got back to the room I probably needed an intervention. My heart rate and blood pressure were sky high. Compressed steam was probably shooting out my ears. I unlocked the door, stepped inside ready to yell at someone or something. Then out of left field Sweet Thang asked: "Who is Webster McDaniels?"

Webster McDaniels was one of Maximillian's friends from Cobalt. Webster sent Maximillian jokes, funny videos (like the Hot-Crazy Matrix) and occasionally (R-rated) adult images. Sweet Thang disapproved of these images and jumped down my throat: "look at all these disgusting e-mails…" Blindsided by this turn of events I started emotionally back pedaling: "I, I, I, I don't look at those e-mails…" Not buying it, Sweet Thang said, "then why was this one opened 17 times?" Shrugging my shoulders, I countered: "Oh that one, I showed it to some of the guys in the lab, they must have reopened it a few times." Steam was now shooting out of her ears. She pointed to the computer screen: "look, look right there (pointing to a message). You said "That's better than ice cream." You love ice cream. You eat ice cream every night." Lesson learned: look and delete.

Moral of the stories: Both ice cream and adult images, at times, can be bad for your health.

In Conclusion

Initially I wrote this book as a Christmas gift for my friends. One of them thought that it would make good reading as many of the stories were pretty funny. By now you can see how fortuitous I was to meet these characters. All friendships started from random circumstances: Turbo and I were both wide receivers in college, Joshua and I were graduate students returning to do undergraduate work, and Maximillian went to the wrong address on his interview visit to Evergreen. For whatever reason, we had an immediate liking for one another and treasured the friendship. As our lives took us to different geographical locations, we continued to appreciate the connection. We still meet for an event at least once a year. Sometimes we race triathlons, sometimes we go skiing, and sometimes we meet for events where we are not actively trying to kill each other like weddings, birthdays or professional sporting events. As the years go by, I am more and more grateful for the opportunity to have met my group of Accidental Friends. I encourage you to reach out to your friends and acknowledge their value. It has been one of the best bucket list items I've ever accomplished, either that or I just recalled the stories fabricated for the first 15 cards of the Rorschach test I took in college.